DATE DUE	RETURNED

Relatively Harmless

Relatively Harmless

Jenny Munday

Playwrights Canada Press
Toronto • Canada

Playwrights Canada Press
The Canadian Drama Publisher
215 Spadina Ave., Suite 230, Toronto, Ontario CANADA M5T 2C7
416.703.0013   fax 416.408.3402
orders@playwrightscanada.com • www.playwrightscanada.com

This book would be twice its cover price were it not for the support of Canadian taxpayers, through the Government of Canada Book Publishing Industry Development Programme, Canada Council for the Arts, Ontario Arts Council, and the Ontario Media Development Corporation.

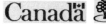

Cover photo "Alley Nightshade" and design: JLArt
Production Editor: MZK

Library and Archives Canada Cataloguing in Publication

Munday, Jenny
    Relatively harmless / Jenny Munday.

A play.
ISBN 978-0-88754-723-2

    I. Title.

PS8576.U496R44 2007   C812'.54   C2007-903780-1

First edition: August 2007.
Printed and bound by Canadian Printco Ltd. at Scarborough, Canada.

In the language of flowers,
the Deadly Nightshades represent Silence,
while the Bittersweet are for Truth.

This work is dedicated to
My Sister,
Allison,
who, although she respected Silence,
did love the Truth.

• ACKNOWLEDGMENTS •

I want to thank the people who helped to bring this script to life, in particular – Live Bait Theatre and its Co-Artistic Directors: Charlie Rhindress and Karen Valanne – who gave me both the opportunity and the obligation (which is what finally made it happen) to finish writing it.

And to:

Sarah Stanley	Don Hannah
Ed MacDonald	John Dartt
Anita Foley	Kay Robertson
Bill MacMillan	June Jarvis
Dave Petersen	Andy McKim
Ilkay Silk	Rick Burns
Paula MacMillan	Glen Nichols
Hannah Grant	David Linkletter

Stephen Rhude and Simone Labuschagne
Theatre New Brunswick and Michael Shamata
Mulgrave Road Theatre and Emmy Alcorn

To the actors and stage managers who participated in workshop readings: Deb Allen, Gay Hauser, Krista Laveck, Dave MacClelland, Michael Pellerin, Craig Wood, Steve Manual, Carol Sinclair, Tara Muise, Emmy, Bill Forbes, Charlie and John, Anne Hardcastle, Mary Ellen MacLean, Kelly Peck, Jane Creaser, Andrew Thomson.

New Brunswick Arts Board   Canada Council for the Arts
Playwrights Atlantic Resource Centre
and
of course,
to those who inspired it and those who made it possible – they know who they are.

Relatively Harmless was first produced by Live Bait Theatre in Sackville, New Brunswick in October 2005 with the following company:

Zoe	Krista Laveck
Donald, the General	John Dartt
Lilith	Gay Hauser
Ben	Ryan Rogerson

Director and Dramaturge: Charlie Rhindress
Lighting Designer: Leigh Ann Vardy
Sound Designer: Krista Wells
Set and Costume Designer: Sean Mulcahy
Stage Manager: Jane Creaser
Choreographer: Krista Laveck
Technical Director: Jocelyn Pringle

Relatively Harmless was presented as a staged reading at the National Arts Centre's On The Verge Series at the Magnetic North Theatre Festival in St. John's, Newfoundland, July 7th, 2006 with the following company:

Zoe	Tracey Ferencz
Donald, the General	Lee J. Campbell
Lilith	Martha Ross
Ben	Anthony Black
Voices	Susan Kent

Director: Leah Cherniak
Dramaturge: Arthur Milner
Sound Designer and Stage Directions: Susan Kent

• CHARACTERS •

The Nightshade Family:

ZOE   A woman in her mid-thirties. When her name is spelled ZOE
– it is pronounced like ZO, one syllable with a long "O" sound.
When it is spelled ZOEY – it is pronounced as two syllables
with a long "E" sound for the second syllable.

DONALD   (or the General) The father. For most of the play, he is
dressed in a "uniform" which is basically a business suit but
evokes a military style uniform and which deteriorates, piece
by piece, over time. NOTE: in scenes that are "post-stroke," all
of the General's movements—all with his right hand—are very
slow and deliberate. When he speaks, sometimes there are
pauses before – sometimes not. When he pauses it's as if he's
trying to focus, or has simply vacated his own premises. After
the stroke, his voice and speech are altered and he sits in
a wheelchair.

LILITH   (or LILY) The wife/mother who dances constantly
throughout the play, except in specified moments. She
continually snaps photographs throughout the play, with
accompanying flashes.

BEN   The younger brother; he is a letter carrier. As time
progresses in the play, his uniform becomes more and more
formal. At first, his Canada Post uniform is the summer
version: short pants; later, the winter version: long pants.

• Time and Place •

The play is set in suburban Toronto during the 1980s and the action
takes place in the present, on the day of the funeral, and in the
past—both recent and distant—stretching over a ten-year period.

• **THE SET** •

The action of the play takes place in several locations: in Zoe's
bachelor apartment in Winnipeg, in a hospital room, in the
General's office, at an airport arrivals area, at a room in the home
of Uncle John and primarily in the various rooms of the
Nightshade home: the General's bedroom and the kitchen, Ben's
basement bedroom and the living/dining room. The Nightshade
home is not realistic in style – it should be almost cartoon-like in
nature, with an absurd, warped quality, indicating that it is off
kilter, out of sync. Zoe's small bachelor apartment, in contrast,
should be very ordered and contained. For instance: a cleanly
styled bed/desk/loft/dresser unit could represent her space.
The set is made up of overlapping flats, made of scrim – allowing
for varied entrances and creating the various playing areas. Some
scenes take place behind scrims; sometimes the flats are used as
screens on which to project images, some of which create other
locations. Movement should flow throughout the play from
one area to another with the use of light and sound so that set
pieces/screens etc. never have to be moved into place. There is
a constant presence—a pall—of smoke in the air, which intensifies
and decreases at various times. There is an almost constant
soundscape present throughout the play. After the General has
the stroke, there is never complete quiet in the Nightshade home.
The sound, or the sound operator, is almost an additional
character in the play and needs to be integrated into the scenes
with that intention/sensibility. Sounds are often exaggerated and
echoed in the soundscape (i.e.: the crash of the vase of flowers,
the crash of the garage door, the roaring, etc.) The soundscape
consists of, among other things: whispering voices (which begin
as indistinguishable words and increase in intensity, only
becoming distinguishable at the end of the play), crashes and
bangs of various types and decibel levels (banging on tables,
doors banging, cupboards opening and closing and banging, a car
crashing into a garage door and other banging), telephone
ringing, feet walking overhead, dishes rattling, kettles whistling
and boiling dry, the General's voice roaring, quiet weeping,
a lion's roar, sobbing, laughing, disembodied offstage voices of
various kinds, clocks ticking and, most importantly, the sound of
the TV – prominent and dominant: rising and lowering in volume

with theme music from various old TV shows that were on
during the 1980s or were in endless re-runs at that time, etc., etc…

Examples/suggestions with regard to TV themes to use:
The themes from shows such as: "The Rockford Files,"
"M.A.S.H.," "Little House on the Prairie," "Night Heat," "Hockey
Night in Canada" theme music (1980s version) and Howie
Meeker's voice, news and weather broadcasts of the time, Blue
Jays' theme song, "Happy Days," "Cagney and Lacey" and other
recognizable TV theme music.

For the original production, a medley of old TV theme music
was used for pre-show music.

Copyrighted materials: Producers are advised that
permission must be sought to use any copyrighted music
suggested in this script (i.e.: TV show themes, songs and/or
music such as: "Puttin' On The Ritz," "Hinterland Who's Who,"
"The Great Escape," "Raindrops Keep Falling on My Head," "My
Devotion," etc.) must be sought for performance rights from the
copyright holder and/or through agencies such as SOCAN.

"M.A.S.H.," the theme from the movie, music by Johnny
Mandel, lyrics by Mike Altman.

The book, *Juggling for the Complete Klutz*, is written by John
Cassidy & B. C. Rimbeaux and is available at most bookstores.

The poems and other words on the walls:

THE DRESSER'S EYES

The green eyes
on the dresser drawers
are watching
me.
I grapple out of
the covers.
But don't turn
my back
in case the
drawers decide
to laugh.

The floor jumps up and
trips me.
The rug wraps its
twisted tail around
my feet.
The door has decided to move and won't let
me find it.
It's playing hide and seek
so I call out
Ollie Ollie Oxen
FREE.
I creep towards
the open pit that
yawns away below.
Will it be easier
to close my
eyes and feel the stairs rise up to me
or
Should I watch
to make sure
the little elves
who come to mend
my clothes for me
aren't sleeping
on the landing?
I wouldn't want to
smoosh them
'cause
I really don't like
to sew.

SPIT IT OUT

Sometimes he doesn't know her name
You can see him hesitate before he speaks
As he tries to recognize the face
To put a label on this other
Then a kind of mumbling
Gurgling, grumbling

ahhh
umm-ing
And then it comes
The name
Sometimes even the right name
With a great effort
Finally able to grasp and meld the concept
The image and The physical power
And SPIT it out.

FOUR DISTINCT FEELINGS

resentment
undifferentiated rage
humiliation
and
guilt.

MY DEVOTION
Sung by Vaughn Monroe

My devotion is endless and deep as the ocean
and, like a star shining from afar, remains forever the same.
My devotion is not just a sudden emotion.
It will be constantly burning
and your love will kindle the flame.
What a sweet beginning to the dream I've planned.
I'm content to be your slave.
And this sensation was never a mere fascination.
Here in my heart, one sweet day it started.
And with time it grew.
My devotion to you.

Scene One

The present. House fades to black as the pre-show music fades out.

In the darkness, we hear whispering VOICES. Almost inaudible at first, they become progressively louder. We can't hear the words the VOICES are whispering; it's a sound that almost sounds like the audience talking before the show. This builds in volume until a loud crash—like a car slamming into a garage door—stops the sound of the whispering VOICES.

Lights up slightly on the GENERAL's bedroom in the Nightshade home on the day of the funeral. In the dimness, we see the outline of a bed, and a bedside table with a lamp. The lights ease up just enough to see that there's a woman sleeping on top of the bed, huddled, wrapped in a blanket. As the whispering VOICES sneak back in again, we hear grunts, snorts, sobs, groans as she is waking out of a nightmare. The whispering VOICES build again and although the words are not really audible, the VOICES are saying: "You're stupid. You're so stupid. You're lazy. You're a loser. You've always been a loser. You're always going to be a loser. Loser. Loser." *They are like a kind of hum of white noise, in which the "Ss" are most prominent. The woman thrashes around, trying to find the light on the wrong side of the bed. She finally finds the light and turns it on. The VOICES stop abruptly. She looks around, trying to figure out where she is, not really awake, although her eyes are wide.*

ZOE   OH GAWD!!! Damn.

Beat.

Damned… weirds. In my… *(She bangs her hand against her forehead.)* Come out *now* ya chicken shits. Come out where I can see ya. Come out and fight! If I could see you, at leas… at least… I could… *(smacks her head again)* Get out!!!

> *She turns the light off and pulls the blanket up over her head as she lies down.*
> *The inaudible whispering VOICES creep back in.*

Damned weirds!

> *The VOICES gain in volume/strength again with the indecipherable buzz of words in a kind of "S" filled background hum.*

(again emerging from under the covers) Okay!!!

> *She turns the light back on and the VOICES fade slightly.*

I give up. Okay?

> *She reaches for a cigarette and lights it. In the soundscape the chorus of whispering VOICES turns into a long, loud sigh of contentment as she exhales: "AAAAAAAHHHHHHHHHH…" Smoke fills the room as the VOICES fade out.*

…disembodied weird voices – bugging me. Can't hide from them anywhere…. Okay! I surrender!

> *Lights shift.*

Scene Two

> *BEN and LILITH are in the kitchen behind one of the scrims. There are flowers and food everywhere. BEN is on the phone, writing in a big notebook. LILITH is dancing furiously. She has an instamatic style camera hanging on a strap around her neck. In the soundscape there is the ambient sound of people in the house after the funeral; a quiet hum of VOICES offstage is present underneath the scene.*
> *ZOE is still in the GENERAL's bedroom, pacing and smoking. She can hear what's going on in the rest of the house.*

LILITH   I told you not to call anyone!

BEN   There are some people we should /

LILITH   I told you not to call – look at all these flowers. People feel they have to… it's not fair.

BEN   Don't you think it's important to /

LILITH   These damned flowers.

> *She deliberately knocks/sweeps a bouquet off the table to the floor, where they "crash" loudly in the soundscape. Pause.*

BEN   The point is… you make them feel good by calling. *(picking up the flowers)* You're letting them know they're important enough to you to let them know.

LILITH   *(stops dancing)* …Oh!

> *She takes a picture of the flowers. They both freeze as they look at each other. In the soundscape, funeral parlour-style music starts to play and the quiet hum of VOICES builds, from which a few specific comments emerge:*

FIRST MOURNER'S VOICE   I used to love your father.

SECOND VOICE   But he wasn't the same man.

ZOE   *(hollering from the bedroom to herself / at the VOICES)* Yeah, brain damage'll do that to a person.

THIRD VOICE   These last years, I haven't known him at all.

ZOE   *(yelling)* Did you ever even see him?

FOURTH VOICE   He just wasn't the same.

ZOE   *(yelling louder)* No kidding!!!

> *She stubs out the cigarette.*

> *In the kitchen, BEN continues to write in the notebook and LILITH continues to dance. During this monologue, the speed of her dancing and the speed of her talking pick up as she goes along, until they are almost in sync, this is the only time in the play that this happens.*

LILITH (*dancing, arranging flowers, arranging food on plates, taking pictures*) We have to make a list of all the dishes that everyone brought and make sure that we get the right dishes back to the right people. Why do people always bring food? Who needs all this food? Who feels like eating anyway?

> *She snaps a photo.*

There's no room for all of this food. Where are we going to put it? Who's going to return all of these damned dishes? I'll have to send thank you notes to everyone. Can you please make sure you've got everyone written down properly?

> *BEN holds the notebook up so she can see what he's been writing – she takes a picture of it.*

Do you think his sisters thought the service was all right? And that brother of his. Showing up late. He never came to see him in the hospital. He only came to see him twice in the ten years he was here – sitting in this house. What is wrong with that family? Was everything okay? Was there enough food? Was the minister all right? Ben, what were you talking about at the end of the service? I couldn't understand what you were saying. Who was that guy who played? Where did Zoey find him? Why did she pick that song? And where is she? Everybody's been looking for her. Everybody wanted to talk to her. Where has she disappeared to? Why does she always pull that disappearing act anyway?

> *Her voice fades out as she dances herself offstage.*

BEN Well, I think we did very well. A pretty good job. We should be pleased with ourselves. Of course it was a lot of work. (*raising his voice to be heard by ZOE*) As the oldest, Zoe, it really should have been your job, but you couldn't be here earlier. We didn't do too badly, but…

> *ZOE groans and crawls under the blanket on the bed to hide.*

Zoe, you were right to insist on his favourite song. The relatives were all very pleased. You did well.

LILITH   *(dancing back on)* Of course, you know what the song is really about don't you? It's all about...

> *ZOE groans loud enough to drown this out. Her groan turns into a roar in the soundscape so that we can't hear LILITH. The groan segues into the opening music and lyrics of the theme from "M.A.S.H." the movie, as smoke wafts into the bedroom and the GENERAL, walking and talking normally, enters the bedroom, wearing Bermuda shorts and a Hawaiian shirt. He listens to the song for a moment.*

GENERAL   I always did like that song.

> *ZOE, scrabbling free of the blanket, screams. The GENERAL, ignoring her, wanders around the room inspecting his various belongings. ZOE screams again, but weakly, almost with a question on the end of it. The GENERAL does not acknowledge her.*

ZOE   Hey! They told me you were dead. *(pause)* Are you dead?

> *He looks at her and winks.*

(running to the door of the room, shouting) Hey! Hey, you guys— he's here—he's okay. Dad /

> *BEN and LILITH (who starts to dance faster) turn on her from the kitchen.*

LILITH   Zoey, for God's sake!

BEN   You're *not* helping.

LILITH   Honestly!

> *LILITH snaps a photo of ZOE, who reacts as if she has been awoken from sleepwalking. They all freeze for a beat.*

GENERAL   Does being at home... now... being in my own house... mean?... Oh.

> *He heaves a great sigh and lies down on the bed.*

In the kitchen, LILITH goes back to dancing and BEN to writing notes. Ignored, ZOE peeks into the bedroom to see if the GENERAL is still there.

ZOE   Do the rest of them know you're not dead – like they don't want anyone else to know? I mean, everybody's here for the funeral and you're hiding in here in the bedroom alive.... What's going on?

No response from the GENERAL.

(yelling to the others) Hey!!!

BEN & LILITH   *(turn toward her and speak together)* Shh! Behave!

ZOE   There's an elephant in the living room!!!

BEN & LILITH   For God's sake.

ZOE   I mean in the bedroom!

BEN & LILITH   Grow up.

ZOE   ELEPHANT!!!

BEN & LILITH   Shut up Zoe!

ZOE   *(to the GENERAL)* Nobody around here ever tells the truth.

There are noises from other parts of the house as murmurs of VOICES and funeral music become more apparent again. ZOE moves cautiously toward the GENERAL on the bed, "keeping her back to the wall," edging closer, she tentatively reaches out to touch him but, instead, reaches for the cigarettes on the table and lights one. Smoke wafts across the stage as she does it and a long drawn out "Aaaahhhhhhhh..." comes from the GENERAL, echoed in the soundscape. He reaches for the cigarette. ZOE backs away as a loud knocking, exaggerated in the soundscape begins. Lights shift as LILITH appears behind the scrim at the door to the bedroom, knocking and dancing.

LILITH   Zoe?

ZOE stares back and forth between the GENERAL and LILITH outside the door. More knocking.

Zoe? *(pause)* Zoey, are you awake? *(pause)* Everybody is
looking for you! *(pause)* Why do you always do this? *(pause)*
Zoe Nightshade, you answer me! *(pause)* Zoe, how long are
you going to stay in there?

ZOE   I don't know.

LILITH   What are you doing?

ZOE   What difference does it make?

LILITH   Are you sleeping?

ZOE   Yeah.

LILITH   You can't stay in there forever.

ZOE   Why not?

LILITH   Because you can't.

ZOE   Why not?

> *Pause. LILITH takes a photo of the door.*

Why not? Seems to be kind of a – a family tradition.

> *She looks at the GENERAL and then back toward the
> door.*

You had a cousin who did. Just went to bed one day and never
got up. He's always been kind of a hero to me. A role model.

LILITH   He was your father's cousin.

ZOE   He was one of the Nightshades?

LILITH   Yes.

ZOE   I always thought he was your cousin. One of the Pollards.

LILITH   Well, he wasn't.

ZOE   Well, that makes sense then.
I guess, sort of…
My name's Nightshade.
I'm part of the Nightshade family.
I grow while I'm sleeping.

LILITH   If you were a tomato, maybe. Besides that only works
   at night when the moon is out.

ZOE   But it's dark in here. It's just like night.
   My brain thinks it's night.
   It's night.
   The longest night.
   The endless night.
   The night of the soul.
   A time to grow.
   Growth is learning.
   I'm learning.
   Try to think of it like that.
   I'm growing, learning, developing myself.
   Expanding. Expanding my horizons. Expanding my soul.
   I'm taking a course.
   I'm going to school. Night school.

LILITH   For God's sake! When did you become so weird?

   She dances/stomps away.

Scene Three

   *Lights shift in a major transition that is reflected in the
   soundscape.*
   *Time warp effects (a theremin or a zither?) indicating
   a time transition to the past, as ZOE moves from the
   bedroom on the day of the funeral to her apartment in
   Winnipeg ten years ago.*

   *A phone rings in ZOE's apartment. As she picks it up,
   lights come up on BEN in the kitchen of the Nightshade
   home.*

ZOE   Hello?

BEN   Hi. Zoe. It's Ben.

ZOE   Ben, how are you? What's up?

BEN   I'm over at the house. Mom called. I think Dad has had
   a couple of little strokes.

*In the soundscape, a barely audible white whispering
noise begins to hum quietly, this is the first time that the
VOICES have appeared for ZOE. This is the precursor
almost to the whispering weird VOICES. The sound
fades in lightly, builds and is out again by the end of the
scene.*

He's sort of been… dozing out for little spaces of time – goes
away kind of – for a few minutes at a time. *(no response, yelling
at her)* Zoe! Zoe are you there?

ZOE *(banging the side of her head to dislodge the sounds, yells into
the phone)* Yeah! I'm here! What did you say?

BEN I think Dad's having small strokes?

ZOE The General?

BEN Yeah. The doctor told him they were muscle spasms.

ZOE A guy like him? Fifty-nine years old, looks eighty, smokes
three packs of cigarettes a day, drinks too much, works too
much, never relaxes and never walks – he gets weird pains
and this doctor tells him he has a muscle spasm?

BEN Or maybe a pinched nerve. Didn't even examine him for
God's sake. Didn't even check his blood pressure.

ZOE And the General believes him, of course?

BEN That's what he wanted to hear, I guess.

ZOE Stupid bugger.

BEN I think he's having little strokes or something.

*Lights out on BEN. The VOICES have built and ZOE
hangs up the phone, rubbing her temple, in response to
the VOICES, as the lights come up behind a scrim wall
on the GENERAL in full uniform, at a desk working,
smoking, drinking coffee. The phone rings, he picks it up
and barks into it:*

GENERAL General Management!!! Nightshade here.

*ZOE salutes him. Lights out on the GENERAL.
Lights shift.*

Scene Four

ZOE picks up the phone at her place and dials while the VOICES hum away at her.

The phone starts to ring in the kitchen of the Nightshade home.
Lights up as BEN enters the kitchen and picks up the phone.

BEN Hello?

ZOE Ben? What are you doing there again?

BEN I just dropped in after /

ZOE I'm coming home for a visit, okay?

BEN Okay.

ZOE You know I've been seeing this counsellor, right?

BEN Yeah. Is it doing you any good?

> *Pause as there is a slight fade up and down of the VOICES.*

ZOE *(reacting to the VOICES)* ...Anyway, I mentioned these little strokes to her when I saw her today and she sits right up and says: "Go home and talk to him. Before it's too late!" I'll be home tomorrow. *(She hangs up.)*

BEN Okay.

> *Lights shift.*

Scene Five

The GENERAL is standing in full uniform, waiting at an airport arrivals area. ZOE enters with a heavy suitcase and purse, sees him and waves.

ZOE Hi! *(He doesn't move.)* Hey!

> *As if he's coming to, he looks up and, in slow motion, lifts his arm slightly and waves. She goes to hug him but*

he doesn't respond – they end up sort of grabbing each others' arms in an awkward embrace.

GENERAL   How was the flight? Only one bag? *(He takes her bag.)* God, what've you got in here? How long are you staying anyway?

An old joke between them.

ZOE   Let me carry it if you're gonna complain that much.

GENERAL   No. No. I've got it.

ZOE   Where's the car?

l to r: Krista Laveck and John Dartt
Photo by Charlie Rhindress

GENERAL   Oh, only about a mile away.

>   *Another old joke.*

ZOE   Of course.

>   *She starts to walk away. He doesn't. She turns back.*

GENERAL   *(as if coming to once more)* So…. Well, we'd better get going. Your mother's waiting at home.

>   *He exits clumsily, listing slightly, with the suitcase. She watches him, then follows.*
>   *Lights shift.*

Scene Six

>   *The GENERAL enters the living/dining room area, carrying a cribbage board and cards. He sits at the table, starts dealing the cards as ZOE follows, carrying drinks, continuing a conversation as she starts to deal the cards.*

ZOE   …it's just that I'd like you to understand what I'm trying to do. I need to find out if I can do it and I need to take the time to figure it out. You know?

>   *They sort their cards.*

GENERAL   How much time do you figure you need?

ZOE   I don't know. I don't want to put a time limit on it.

GENERAL   What's wrong with a time limit. *(pause)* I know what I'm going to do with the rest of my life.

ZOE   What?

GENERAL   I've got about six years left to put in before I can get out of damned middle management and let those smart-ass, university-educated know-nothings, take my job – the job I trained them to do.

ZOE   You hate your job, don't you?

GENERAL   It's just a job.

> *He tosses two cards into the crib and cuts the deck,*
> *holding them and waiting for her to toss cards into the*
> *crib then picks up the top card and turns it over.*

It'll be my turn soon.

ZOE   Hold your horses – it's my crib.

GENERAL   *(He leads.)* Seven. I'm going to take early retirement and go to Western University and study history.

ZOE   You're kidding. History? *(She plays a card.)* Fifteen for two. *(She pegs.)* When did you decide this?

GENERAL   I always wanted to study history. *(tosses a card into play)* Twenty-four for three. *(He pegs.)* Always was interested in history.

ZOE   Go. Why?

GENERAL   Thirty-one for two. *(He pegs.)* It would be good to know why things happened the way they did, don't you think?

ZOE   Why Western?

> *They continue to play.*

GENERAL   Always liked London. I went there once on a business trip. It's a pretty town. It's not Toronto. It's quiet. Classy.

ZOE   *(playing)* Seven.

GENERAL   Fifteen for two. *(He pegs.)*

ZOE   *(playing cards one on top of the other)* Twenty-two, twenty-seven. One for last card. *(She pegs.)*

GENERAL   You know, Zoe, you shouldn't worry so much about what you're going to do. *(picking up his cards and counting)* Fifteen two, fifteen four, and eight is twelve and one for the jack is thirteen. *(He pegs.)* You want to work in an office all day and write poetry all night – that's fine. I just don't know why you have to do it in Winnipeg.

ZOE   I always liked Winnipeg. It's not Toronto. It's quiet.

GENERAL   Ha! You'll be fine.

ZOE   *(Staring at him, she counts her cards and pegs.)* Fifteen two, fifteen four. *(She picks up her crib as he gathers up the other cards and starts to shuffle.)* Fifteen two, fifteen four and?…

GENERAL   *(He grabs the cards from her, looks at them, shoves them into the deck he is shuffling.)* …And the rest don't score. *(He laughs.)*

> *Lights shift.*

Scene Seven

> *The phone rings in ZOE's apartment, and rings and rings as lights come up on BEN in his room in the basement of the Nightshade home. Finally, the lights come up on ZOE sleeping. She wakes up and fumbles for the phone.*

BEN   It's Ben. Dad's in the hospital. He's had a massive stroke.

> *Pause.*
> *In the soundscape, the white noise whispering weird VOICES begin to hum quietly as the GENERAL wanders into the kitchen, stunned, his left side dragging a little bit, unsteady. The whispering VOICES intensify in volume.*

ZOE   Dad?

LILITH   *(coming into the kitchen behind him – walking normally)* Donald?

> *He doesn't respond. He walks toward the wall, stops when he gets there, facing it. Then he tries to keep going, smashes into the wall and topples over on his left side.*

Donald!!!

> *As he falls, she starts to dance. She bends over him, then runs/dances to the phone and starts to dial as the lights fade on the GENERAL and LILITH.*

BEN   He's had a stroke.

ZOE   Oh God.... How bad is it?

BEN   We don't know yet.

ZOE   Should I come right home?

BEN   I don't know.

ZOE   Yeah, but /

BEN   There's nothing you can do.

VOICES increase.

ZOE   Okay. Well, you'll keep me posted? You'll call me then?

BEN   I'll call.

ZOE   Can he talk?

BEN   We don't know yet.

ZOE   ...so... how is *she?*

BEN   I don't know.

ZOE   ...yeah. I'll call her later... later tonight then... yeah.

BEN   Fine.

ZOE   You'll have to let me know how things... she won't tell me the truth – so you'll have to let me know.

BEN   Okay.

Pause as the VOICES rise slightly again.

ZOE   Is he gonna die?

Pause.

BEN   I don't know.

ZOE   Oh geesus. Well, call me... I'll – I'll – I don't know... I don't know what to do. I don't... *(Breathing like she's crying but she's not, she wanders in circles.)* I can't – I mean I'm not there right? There's nothing I can do, so...

BEN hangs up the phone. ZOE stands listening to the dial tone as the VOICES rise in volume again, then fade

*out as lights shift to the GENERAL in the hospital
behind a scrim.*

Scene Eight

*The GENERAL in bed. He wakes up, coming out of
sleep serenely. We can see him peacefully asleep, waking
up very gently, smiling – a satisfied sigh. His eyes open.
He looks around awkwardly, which shocks him, he
becomes more and more disoriented and frightened as he
tries to move and discovers that he is paralysed on his
left side, he fumbles and panics. He screams – his speech
is altered:*

GENERAL   CHRIST! *(pause)* LILITH!

Pause. He fumbles around, struggles and yells.

LILITH!!! SOMEBODY!!! SOMEBODY! ONE OF YOU!

*He falls out of bed, lands on the floor – half frozen,
moaning.*

LILITH   *(offstage)* What do you mean? Nurse? Where are you
going? What's happened?

*She dances quick-step into the room, then stops,
stunned. Then she dances all around the GENERAL in
repeated futile, ineffectual attempts to help him, while he
continues to groan. BEN runs in.*

BEN   Jesus! What's going on?

LILITH   Donald… he… fell… he fell… he /

BEN   Fell? What was he doing? Was he trying to get out of bed?
(moving to help the GENERAL)

LILITH   I don't know. The nurse just left. She said she couldn't
lift him by herself. She has a bad back and she's pregnant.
(BEN freezes.) She wouldn't lift him. She left.

BEN   I'm going to find a damned orderly. *(exits)*

3333453333233334333

LILITH dances over to try to help him. She accidentally kicks him.

GENERAL OW! OW! OW!

She accidentally grabs him by the hair, then accidentally twists his arm.

OW! OW! OW!

BEN *(coming back into the room)* I couldn't find an orderly. I couldn't find a nurse. I can't find anybody.

He grabs the GENERAL's bad side, trying to get him up on the bed, while LILITH dances around.

Come on, Dad. *(as he tries to lift him)*

GENERAL I have to go. I have to go. I have to go.

ZOE enters into the room, carrying a suitcase, unseen by the others.

LILITH The nurse told you not to worry about it.

GENERAL That's NOT…

LILITH *(to BEN)* They've got him in Depends.

ZOE That's not what he means.

LILITH *(stops dancing)* So, you're finally here.

BEN How do you know what he means?

The white noise VOICES come in immediatelly – they are now travelling with ZOE all the time, though their words are still indistinguishable.

ZOE Does anybody work here?

She helps BEN move the GENERAL to the bed. LILITH starts dancing again.

BEN Come on, Dad. Lift your butt.

They struggle to get him up on the bed.

We're going to have to take care of him ourselves.

>*He takes hold of sleeping restraints attached to the bed and starts to put them on him. The GENERAL protests weakly.*

ZOE   Do you have to do that?

>*LILITH has her hands over her face: at her mouth (stifling a scream?), they move slowly to cover her eyes, then her ears.*

BEN   They told us it would help ease the strain on his arm and help keep him safe – so he won't fall out of bed again. You just place the strap here and attach the buckle.

ZOE   Do you have to tie him up?

BEN   That's what they told us to do to keep him safe. Do you want him to fall again?

ZOE   Stop it!

>*She starts to move to stop him. LILITH holds her back.*

We have to help him.

>*As BEN deals with the straps, LILITH lets go of ZOE and starts to dance around and try to help.*

BEN   *(to LILITH)* Just let me *show* you. Listen to me.

>*LILITH continues to dance and ineffectually try to help and keeps getting in the way.*

(to LILITH) Just listen! *(to ZOE)* Can't you help?

>*ZOE wraps her arms around LILITH to hold her still. LILITH freezes. There are little staccato taps of her feet as she is being held in place and can't really dance.*

GENERAL   OW! OW! OW! Ooooooooh. Somebody.

ZOE   These restraint things are horrible. We shouldn't use them.

BEN   I'm just /

ZOE   I know – you're just trying to do the right thing. You always do.

BEN   I'm just doing what the doctors and nurses told us to do.

GENERAL   Somebody. One of you!

ZOE   Even so. Shouldn't a nurse or an orderly or someone be doing this?

BEN   All the nurses ever say to him is:

> *He imitates the nurses' voices and LILITH whispers it along with him.*

"Now try to stop complaining, Mr. Nightshade. You're disturbing the other patients."

> *LILITH, imitating the nurses' voices, BEN whispers it along with her.*

LILITH   "Now try to stop complaining, Mr. Nightshade. You're disturbing the other patients."

> *The imitated voices echo in the soundscape. The GENERAL starts to cry. They all freeze.*

ZOE   What can we do, Dad? What do you want?

GENERAL   I want to die.

> *They freeze. LILITH stops dancing and moves toward the bed and leans over to hug him.*

Get away! Get away!

> *LILITH dances away from the bed, dancing in a kind of stunned trance.*

BEN   I never saw him cry before.

GENERAL   I'm not an animal.

ZOE   What?

GENERAL   I was afraid I was gonna die.

BEN   What?

GENERAL   Now, I'm afraid I'm not.

LILITH   Oh God.

She stops dancing again. BEN leaves the hospital room. ZOE moves over to LILITH who is standing very still. ZOE reaches out to touch her but doesn't. LILITH keeps her back to ZOE.

GENERAL   Nobody's listening!!!

The lights fade over the GENERAL's bed.

ZOE   You okay?

LILITH   All the things we were going to do. All the things we never did.

ZOE puts her arms around her.

We never will.

She shakes ZOE off and starts to dance just a little. Lights shift and fade on the hospital room.

Scene Nine

ZOE joins BEN in the room in the basement of the Nightshade home.

ZOE   He seems – just – inaccessible – half paralyzed and who knows how far gone inside.

BEN   …and, I guess, so is she…

ZOE   We've got to do something. We've got to help him. The doctors aren't doing anything.

The lights come up slightly on the GENERAL and LILITH in the hospital. She is still dancing in her trance-like state and the GENERAL, his uniform deteriorating, is sitting in a wheelchair, very slumped, an arm brace on his left side which is drooping, while he raises and lowers his hand in slow motion, trying to squeeze a rubber ball in his left hand.

Nobody's helping. They won't even answer questions. We have to *do* something.

BEN   I knew you'd behave this way.

*The hum/hiss of the white noise VOICES comes in
quickly – the words almost becoming audible.*

ZOE What's that supposed to mean?

BEN You haven't been here since the beginning. You don't
know what's going on. What is it you think we can do?

ZOE I don't know – something.

BEN He's got to help himself.

ZOE He can't and she's a mess.

BEN They have to figure it out themselves.

*The lights begin to fade out on LILITH and the
GENERAL in the hospital.*

ZOE He's covered in bruises. They let him fall. We should sue.

BEN That would help a lot! I'll bet that would make the doctors
more helpful. Listen, they say he'll be in the hospital til the
acute phase is past. They say they're putting together a team
to assess his needs. They say he'll go to rehab…

ZOE Team? You think these idiots are capable of putting
together a team to help him? They don't care. They don't like
him.

Pause.

I dreamt last night that we came to the hospital and they'd cut
off his legs. They didn't even tell us – just cut off his legs and
put him in this small room down the hall and shut the door.

Pause.

BEN Why don't you go home? Why don't you just go home.
You can't help.

*Blast of the white noise VOICES in the soundscape as
BEN exits.*

ZOE …so. I guess I'll go home.

Lights shift with sound, the VOICES and smoke.

Scene Ten

ZOE is in her bed at her apartment, with the blanket over her head as the VOICES build and build to the sound of the car crashing into the garage door.

Circus music starts to play as the lights come up on BEN behind the scrim wall in ZOE's room. He's wearing a top hat and wielding a set of bongo drums which he plays to the beat of the music. Shocked awake, ZOE pulls the blanket down to see what is going on. The GENERAL (in full uniform) and LILITH dance in.

BEN *(wielding the top hat and bongoes and speaking in the voice of a ringmaster)* Ah yes, ladies and gentlemen, the Deadly Nightshades have taken the floor once again.

The GENERAL and LILITH lie down on top of ZOE in the bed.

A family of plants!!! The genus solanum!

ZOE *(struggling under their weight)* They're poisonous.

BEN Deadly! The Deadly Nightshades! Sometimes only soporific! They're relatively harmless.

ZOE *(crawling out from under LILITH and the GENERAL)* And sometimes they're relatives but not necessarily harmless.

BEN But some are only slightly poisonous, like – potatoes. *Maestro!* Please.

He does a drum roll on the bongoes singing:

I say potato. *(long vowel sound)*
You say potato. *(the short vowel sound)*
I say tomato. *(the long vowel sound)*
And you say…*(indicating to ZOE that the next line is hers)*

ZOE *(reluctantly, not singing)* Tomato. *(the short vowel sound)*

BEN *(singing – the long vowel sound)* Potato.

ZOE *(not singing – the short vowel sound)* Potato.

The GENERAL and LILITH join in.

GENERAL   *(singing)* Tomato. *(long vowel)*

LILITH   *(singing)* Tomato. *(short vowel)*

BEN & LILITH & GENERAL   *(singing together)* "Let's call the whole thing off."

> *The original jingle from the Chiquita Banana commercial begins to play. BEN starts to play the bongo drums wildly, while LILITH and the GENERAL get up and start dancing. LILITH puts a Carmen Miranda-type hat, with bananas on it, on her head. She and the GENERAL do the cha-cha while they and BEN sing the Chiquita Banana song along with the recording:*

"Hello Amigos!
I'm Chi-qui-ta Ba-na-na and I've come to say
Ba-na-nas have to rip-en in a cer-tain way."

ZOE   *(standing up on the bed)* Welcome to the Banana Factory where everybody in the Nightshade family has a role to play!

> *She gets back under the covers but keeps peeking out at them to watch the others continue to sing the banana song and dance.*

BEN & LILITH & GENERAL   *(singing together)* "When they are fleck'd with brown and have a gold-en hue,
Ba-na-nas taste the best, and are the best for you.
You can put them in a sa-lad
You can put them in a pie-aye—
An-y way you want to eat them
It's im-pos-si-ble to beat them.
But ba-na-nas like the cli-mate of the ve-ry, ve-ry tro-pi-cal e-qua-tor.
So you should nev-er put ba-na-nas in the re-frig-er-ra-tor.
Cha-Cha-Cha."

> *A crescendo – then abrupt shift of music and lights.*
> *BEN disappears from behind the scrim, we can still hear the bongoes as they fade off.*
> *ZOE collapses back on the bed.*
> *As the GENERAL and LILITH dance off, a phone rings.*

*Lights come up on the GENERAL's office. The
GENERAL dances into the office space, wearing the
Carmen Miranda hat. The phone rings again, he picks it
up and barks into it:*

GENERAL   General Management! Nightshade here.

Lights shift.

Scene Eleven

*ZOE, in her apartment, picks up the phone and dials.
It rings in the basement space in the Nightshade home
where BEN is sitting on the futon, reading* Juggling for
the Complete Klutz. *He picks the phone up on the first
ring.*

BEN   Hello?

ZOE   Ben?

BEN   Yeah.

ZOE   You're there?

BEN   Yeah. *(pause)* What's up?

ZOE   A friend of mine was here the other day. His mother just
died.

BEN   Oh?

ZOE   We were talking and at one point, I guess I said – "Yeah,
I know, my Dad died last year too."

BEN   Jesus, Zoe. He's not dead yet.

ZOE   I know. I didn't even know I'd said it until my friend said:
"Oh, I'm sorry. I didn't know your father died." *(pause)*
Neither did I, 'til then.

*Pause as the VOICES in the soundscape start to fade in,
building and fading through the course of the scene.*

I was thinking—maybe I should—maybe I could come for
a visit soon.

BEN   Oh? You can get away from work?

>   *He picks up three small square beanbags and starts to juggle them. More VOICES.*

ZOE   I guess they can always hire another short-term office temp.

BEN   What about your other work?

ZOE   I guess I can bring some with me to work on. Supposedly you can write anywhere. Or so they say.

BEN   How's it going anyway? Had anything published yet?

>   *More VOICES.*

ZOE   …Uh… a bit of a crisis of confidence at the moment, I guess.

BEN   What's that mean?

ZOE   I've submitted some things. Nobody's interested so far.

>   *More VOICES.*

BEN   Oh.

ZOE   How are you?

BEN   I'm fine.

ZOE   How's school?

BEN   I quit.

>   *More VOICES.*

ZOE   What? Why?

BEN   I got on full time at the post office. It's good. It's easier on the head.

ZOE   Oh. Are you sure?

BEN   Yes. I'm sure.

>   *Pause. More VOICES.*

ZOE   So, what else is /

BEN   Mom's got a Red Cross homemaker coming in once a week so she can get out of the house.

> *He starts to juggle faster.*

Sometimes, apparently, we could even get a nurse in for a week or so, so she could get away for longer. Once a week they get a meal from Meals on Wheels. I'm staying here now.

ZOE   Staying there?

BEN   I gave up my apartment. Moved back in here.

ZOE   What?

> *Pause as BEN concentrates on the juggling.*

BEN   I've started doing some volunteer work.

ZOE   Really?

> *No response as he continues to try to juggle.*

With who? For what?

BEN   Oh you know – the Red Cross, Meals on Wheels, at the Seniors' Centre, stuff like that.

> *More VOICES.*

ZOE   Oh. *(pause)* You trying to get the system to work for you or something?

BEN   Ha! Yeah. Fat chance, eh?

> *Pause. More VOICES.*

Might be nice if you came to visit. She'd like that. He'd probably like to see you.

ZOE   I don't know. Whenever I'm around, things don't go all that well. I just seem to interfere with all the rhythms.

BEN   Nah. That's just 'cause you're not here enough. You have to stay long enough to – you know – get into it.

> *He grabs the beanbags out of the air and stops juggling. More VOICES as the lights shift.*

Scene Twelve

> *The introductory instrumental section of "My Devotion" begins to play. The GENERAL, in full dress uniform, dances into the Nightshade's living/dining room, with LILITH. Surprised, ZOE moves over to watch them. LILITH "steps out" and ZOE starts dancing with the GENERAL.*

ZOE   I used to love to dance with you. You were a good dancer. When I was a kid, I used to stand on top of your feet while you did the dancing. Remember?

> *She stands on his feet and they dance. LILITH comes back, ZOE "steps out" and the GENERAL and LILITH continue to dance as the music swells and segues into "Puttin' on the Ritz" as sung by Gene Wilder in the movie "Young Frankenstein" as the GENERAL and LILITH perform a dance routine. Pieces of the GENERAL's uniform start to fall off as they spin around. The music switches into the version of the song as sung/brayed by Peter Boyle as the Monster in "Young Frankenstein." The GENERAL's posture and demeanour revert to the stroke victim. As BEN steps in and hands the GENERAL a cane, more pieces of his uniform fly off. The GENERAL and LILITH, no longer dancing, are walking down the hall, to bed. He is leaning on his cane, hobbling. She's dancing, trying to help, she almost trips him.*

GENERAL   *(waving the cane around erratically and roaring, almost toppling over)* Get out of the way!

> *As LILITH dances away, ZOE moves toward him and walks him to the bed, with LILITH dancing along behind. ZOE gets him to sit on the bed and takes the cane away.*

ZOE   Okay?

> *She helps him get his jacket off.*

GENERAL   Ow! Ow! Ow! Ow!

ZOE   Sorry. Sorry. Sorry.

GENERAL   Be careful!

ZOE   Okay. Lie down now.

> *The GENERAL tries to lie down, loses balance, starts to topple – can't get his leg up on the bed.*

GENERAL   My leg! My leg!

> *ZOE lifts his leg up for him. LILITH and ZOE, together, get him lying down.*

Yeah.

> *LILITH dances out and ZOE follows.*

ZOE   Goodnight.

LILITH   *(dancing back in to turn off the light)* Goodnight.

> *She dances off stage.*

GENERAL   *(with a big sigh, then very definite)* Goodnight, ladies!

> *There is a light shift.*

ZOE   *(moving into BEN's basement room)* It's like this every night?

> *BEN in his space, juggling the beanbags. LILITH from offstage.*

BEN & LILITH   Every night.

> *The white noise VOICES hum softly.*

ZOE   It's hard to remember sometimes – he does have some good points.

BEN   He's full of contradictions.

ZOE   Full of fear. And confidence.

BEN   Demanding.

ZOE   Generous.

BEN   A bully.

ZOE   A hero. Remember the time when he and that friend of his – that guy he worked with – they chased a robber down a street in Montreal and helped get the guy arrested. And that time when he rescued a guy whose car went into the St. Lawrence River while Mom and the Hansens watched?

BEN   *(stops juggling)* You know, I read somewhere recently that there's actually a law in Quebec that obligates you to try to rescue someone in trouble. The Rescue Law, it's called. I wonder if that's true.

ZOE   I wonder if he knew that at the time.

BEN   I always thought he was like John Wayne. He isn't. Wasn't. But I always thought he was. I think because of that movie – "True Grit" – you know the part where John Wayne falls off his horse and says "We'll camp *here*?"

ZOE   "Pilgrim."

BEN   That's him. And then John Wayne's never wrong, ever. He used to be like that.

ZOE   All of a sudden, he's never right.

BEN   Yeah.

> *He starts to juggle again.*
> *Lights shift.*

Scene Thirteen

> *Lights up on the GENERAL sitting at the table in the living/dining room, in the wheelchair in his deteriorating uniform, very slumped, arm brace on his left side, which is drooping. An unlit cigarette in his mouth, he is trying to endorse a cheque, with his signature. LILITH, holding another cheque for him to sign, is standing beside him.*

GENERAL   Shit! *(as the cheque slips away from him)* Jesus Christ! Jesus Christ! Hold it. Move the goddamned ashtray out of the way.

He tries to move it but turns it over. LILITH starts trying to clean up, hold the cheque for him and calm him down. Both cheques end up on the table at once.

LILITH The $800 one is made out to Donald Nightshade, that's the one you have to sign first.

He makes a grab for the second cheque.

No, that's the $300 cheque. *(grabbing it away)* That's made out to General Nightshade. *(switching the cheques around)* The $800 one – just sign it Donald Nightshade. Sign it.

GENERAL Which one am I signing? *(as he signs it)*

LILITH *(lookng at the signature on one of them)* It's pretty good. You just don't practice enough.

She takes a photo of it.

GENERAL It's as good as any doctor's signature.

He signs the second cheque.

There! If it's not good enough then you can't cash it and then you won't get any more of my money!!

He throws the pen across the room.

LILITH Donald, really. *(She dances over and picks up the pen.)* There's no need to holler. I'm only trying to /

GENERAL Make me a coffee and leave me alone!!!

LILITH starts humming and dances off. The GENERAL gets hold of the remote and flicks through the channels, with the sound blaring, landing on the instrumental TV theme music for "M.A.S.H."
ZOE is in the kitchen, starting to head out the door.
BEN comes into the kitchen, carrying the newspaper.

BEN Hey! Where you going?

ZOE Out.

BEN Where?

ZOE Just out!

BEN Oh.

ZOE I've got to get out of here!

BEN You just got here yesterday.

> *TV sound blares again as the GENERAL is trying to adjust the remote.*

Can you remember when the only time he ever watched TV was—

ZOE "Hockey Night in Canada."

BEN Or on Sundays when we all watched "Walt Disney," "Ed Sullivan" and then "Bonanza" together. Remember that?

ZOE Now it's all day, all night, non-stop TV. How can she stand it? I can't take it anymore. If I hear that "M.A.S.H." theme one more time…

BEN Whoever knew you could come to hate Alan Alda so much? *(pause)* Listen, you mind if I go out with you?

> *The "M.A.S.H." theme blares again and then diminishes as the GENERAL is again struggling to adjust the remote.*

GENERAL Ben!!!

BEN Oh Christ. Not again!

GENERAL BEN!!!

BEN Son of a bitch! The stupid bastard. He's so *fucking stupid*. He doesn't know anything. He can't do anything. He just sits there all day. He's no good for anything. He sits there all day and never says anything – never needs anything. Then just when you're all ready to go out the door he yells: "BEN!"

> *He throws the newspaper on the table.*

WHAT?

GENERAL I gotta take a leak.

BEN JESUS CHRIST. EVERY FUCKING TIME!

ZOE Jesus, Ben, take it easy. You go on out. I can /

BEN   HE'S CRAZY. The useless bastard.

> *BEN exits, the door slams and echoes in the soundscape.*

GENERAL   What's that banging???

ZOE   *(going into the living/dining room)* …uh… Ben just… went /

GENERAL   He's always banging and slamming. He's wrecking my house! Why does he bother coming here if he's going to act like that and WRECK MY HOUSE!

ZOE   I'll help you, Dad.

GENERAL   Help what? What do you want?

ZOE   I thought you needed to go to the bathroom.

GENERAL   What are you talking about?

> *Pause. He picks up his watch and looks at it.*

What time is it?

ZOE   *(Confused, she looks at her watch.)* Uh, four o'clock, why?

GENERAL   Where's the remote? Gimme the remote. "Rockford's" on.

> *LILITH begins to dance behind the scrim – in the kitchen.*
> *As ZOE watches, the GENERAL grabs the remote from the table, where he left it, and concentrating intently switches from channel to channel, as the soundscape switches back and forth between different show themes – getting louder and louder until it finally lands on the "Rockford Files" theme.*

Got it. What are you looking at? What do you want?

> *Lights shift up slightly on LILITH in the kitchen, dancing and reading the newspaper. BEN is sitting with his head in his hands on the futon in the basement. ZOE takes a booklet titled: "Stroke: Why Do They Act That Way?" out of her purse and crosses to BEN, hands him the booklet, tips her hand in a gesture of farewell and*

> *exits with a loud banging of the door in the soundscape.*
> *There are, at this point, no VOICES in the soundscape.*

What's that banging?

> *LILITH continues to dance in place with the newspaper.*
> *While BEN reads from the book the theme music from*
> *CBC TV's original "Hinterland's Who's Who" starts to*
> *play.*

BEN *(reading from the booklet "Stroke: Why Do They Act That*
Way?") "If a stroke patient is able to speak, understand speech
and even read, he is often thought to be unimpaired. Spatial-
perceptual abilities are as important as speech but they tend
to be performed automatically and are therefore easily
overlooked. It is easy to overestimate the abilities of the left
hemiplegic when he encounters difficulties with what appear
to be simple tasks, he may be regarded as uncooperative, or
even unpleasant. Divide duties so that the burden of care does
not fall on one person. Help the patient take responsibility for
doing his exercises regularly, for self care and other activities.
Praise any successful effort that he makes."

> *Lights shift down on BEN as the music fades out.*

Scene Fourteen

> *Lights up on the GENERAL, in his chair at the table,*
> *and ZOE watching TV together. LILITH dances into the*
> *room to dance in place behind the GENERAL. She*
> *points to the newspaper as she spreads it out on the table*
> *in front of him.*

LILITH   Harold Banbury!

> *She snaps a photo of the paper.*

ZOE   Who's he?

GENERAL   Harold Banbury!

LILITH   He died.

ZOE   Who was he?

GENERAL   He sang at our wedding.

LILITH   Forty years ago!

GENERAL   Oh yeah.

ZOE   What did he sing?

> *Pause as the GENERAL and LILITH make eye contact and start to sing together.*

LILITH & GENERAL   "My devotion is endless and deep as the ocean
and, like a star shining from afar, remains forever the same."

LILITH   "What a sweet beginning to the dream I've planned."

GENERAL   *(struggling to find the words)* "…constantly burning …your love will kindle the flame."

LILITH   "I'm content to be your slave."

GENERAL   Your wish is my command.

LILITH   "My devotion is not just a sudden emotion."

GENERAL   "…it started.
And with time it grew."

LILITH & GENERAL   "My devotion to you."

> *Pause as they look at each other before they both burst into roars of laughter at the irony of it all. He starts to cough and choke, still laughing. LILITH automatically and repeatedly pounds him on the back, as the instrumental version of "My Devotion" drifts in, then out off the soundscape.*

ZOE   Dad, how did you feel when you had your stroke?

GENERAL   *(instantly in a rage)* What the hell kind of a question is that? What are you talking about? What do you mean?

ZOE   I was reading about a man who had a stroke. He described it and I wondered. I mean, how did you feel? What were your feelings?

l to r: Gay Hauser and John Dart
Photo by Charlie Rhindress

GENERAL   I can't remember.

Silence.

LILITH   You weren't unconscious ever, were you?

ZOE   What happened?

GENERAL   I don't know. I got up and walked out here to the kitchen wall, didn't I?

LILITH   I know what I saw.

ZOE   Then what happened?

LILITH   He fell.

ZOE   Dad, do you remember falling?

GENERAL   I walked to the wall. That's all I know. I don't REMEMBER!!!

ZOE   I wonder how you felt.

LILITH   Me too – I always wondered how you felt...

Silence.

GENERAL   Are you gonna make me some more coffee?

> *LILITH dances out to the kitchen where the phone immediatelly starts to ring.*

Lilith!

> *LILITH picks up the phone and starts to talk in her "company" voice.*

LILITH   Hello? Oh yes, hello, John.

GENERAL   Lilith!!

LILITH   How are you… and Sarah?

GENERAL   *(to ZOE)* She can't hear me now. This house isn't that big! She's right there in the next room and she can't hear me.

LILITH   Oh, everything's fine here. Yes, Zoey is visiting…

GENERAL   She can never hear me. I can hear her on the phone now. Why can't she hear me?

> *Lights shift.*

Scene Fifteen

> *ZOE and BEN are in BEN's room in the basement.*
>
> *LILITH is busy in the kitchen, opening and closing cupboards, doing dishes, etc. She is humming "My Devotion" to herself.*
>
> *The GENERAL is sitting at the table in the living/ dining room. Various elements of the soundscape are very present: noises of TV, kitchen cupboard doors banging, etc. The sound should produce a sense of bedlam in the house.*

LILITH   Why can't you /

GENERAL   I can't help it.

ZOE   Let's do something.

BEN   Okay. *(pause)* What?

ZOE   I don't know.

GENERAL   It's just the way I am!!!

LILITH   Donald, be quiet. The neighbours.... There's no need /

GENERAL   I'm the boss here!

> *TV sounds increase.*

BEN   We can't.

ZOE   Why?

> *Kitchen cupboard doors slamming.*

GENERAL   Stop that banging!!

> *Footsteps in the soundscape.*

BEN   I don't know. We just can't.

ZOE   Why not? Why can't we? Why can't we ever do anything? It's like we're always waiting for something. What are we waiting for?

BEN   God only knows.

> *He picks up the beanbags off the futon and starts to juggle. Noises from other parts of the house increase. Lights shift.*

Scene Sixteen

> *ZOE is alone somewhere in the house, while LILITH, in the kitchen, is dancing away slowly and quietly, fairly content, in her own world, in her head, humming quietly to herself over the TV sounds in the soundscape. The GENERAL is absorbed in the TV. BEN is in his space juggling. A loud banging noise—like a big fist on a table—starts to resound through the house, in the soundscape.*

ZOE   *(She has her head in her hands clutching her hair.)* THERE'S AN ELEPHANT IN THE LIVING ROOM!!!

LILITH keeps dancing – speeding up, shaking her head and holding her finger to her lips and sshhhhhhing. She tries to hum louder at the same time. BEN juggles faster. while the banging noise comes again. The GENERAL cranks the volume on the TV.

ELEPHANT!!!

Banging noise once again, LILITH speeds up, shushing, moves to the window, looks out to see if anyone saw/ heard, shuts curtains, makes sure doors are closed, dancing frantically, shushing and shaking her head and starting to sing. She dances back behind the scrim and disappears. BEN starts to whistle the same tune that LILITH is singing and walks out of his room, juggling.

(in a whisper/sob) Elephant...

She starts to bang the back of her head against the wall, and the soundscape kicks in to make it a very loud banging.

GENERAL   What's that banging?

Lights shift.

Scene Seventeen

ZOE is in BEN's room, waiting. BEN enters.

ZOE   Well?

BEN   The doctor says he's as well as can be expected. There's really nothing he can do.

ZOE   And her?

BEN   She has to stay off her feet for awhile. She's worn out.

ZOE   Did he tell her that?

BEN   Yes, but we can't force her.

ZOE   Did he tell him? He's the one who has to know.

BEN   He said: "What do you expect from me? I can't solve all of their problems."

ZOE   And you said?

BEN   I said: "What can you do, Doctor?"

ZOE   To which, he replied?

BEN   To which there was no reply.

ZOE   Oh.

BEN   What a surprise, eh?

ZOE   It was a year after the stroke that she ran over her foot with the lawn mower and just about cut off her big toe, right?

BEN   Yeah, you came home that time and stayed for three weeks.

> *He picks up the beanbags and starts to juggle, while in the soundscape, the murmuring "S" filled VOICES drift in.*

ZOE   The next year she took skiing lessons for the first time in her life and fell and broke her leg, right?

BEN   Yeah. You didn't come home that time.

> *More VOICES.*

She was in a cast and couldn't do anything for months.

> *More VOICES.*

ZOE   The next year, she left the car in gear and went and got herself between it and the garage, right?

> *A loud crash – the sound of a car slamming into a garage door.*

BEN   Yeah, she was black and blue all over and couldn't walk right for awhile. It cost $2000 to fix the garage door.

> *More VOICES.*

ZOE   You think maybe she might be trying to tell us something?

BEN   Well, the accidents have stopped. She seems to have gotten used to things.

ZOE   It is year six.

BEN   No wonder she's worn out.

ZOE   When did she start taking the pictures?

BEN   It was after the garage door incident.

ZOE   I guess taking pictures of everybody and everything instead of actually engaging is one way of coping.

> *More VOICES.*

BEN   It's certainly made for some pretty blurry pictures.

> *Lights shift.*

Scene Eighteen

> *The soundscape kicks in with TV sounds. The GENERAL is at the table, smoking and reading. LILITH dances in, puts a coffee cup on the table beside him, approaching him from his bad side and startling him. He jumps.*

GENERAL   Quit aggravating me!!!

> *She snaps a photo of him. He reacts to the flash, then closes the book and takes his reading glasses off and just sits there. LILITH dances back out.*

> *Lights up on BEN in his space, sitting with his head in his hands and on ZOE at her place, sitting with her head in her hands, while the VOICES hum around her head.*

BEN   She doesn't seem to be able to remember to always approach him from his good side so she doesn't startle him.

> *The GENERAL starts to call LILITH but stops himself.*

> *ZOE stops clutching her head and starts to write on the walls of her apartment.*

ZOE   Sometimes he doesn't know her name.
You can see him hesitate before he speaks
As he tries to recognize the face
To put a label on this "other."

> *LILITH dances back in with a sandwich on a plate. She starts toward his left side, stops herself and approaches from his right side. The GENERAL stares at her as if he's never seen her before.*

Then a kind of mumbling
Gurgling, grumbling.

GENERAL   *(He starts to grumble, gurgle.)* …Ahhhhh…
ummmmm…

ZOE   An… ahh… umming

> *And then with a great effort it comes.*

GENERAL   LILITH!

> *LILITH jumps and drops the plate, dances around picking up the sandwich, takes a picture of the sandwich and dances out.*

ZOE   The name
Sometimes even the right name
With a great effort
Finally able to grasp and meld the concept
The image and the physical power
And SPIT it out.

> *LILITH dances out.*

BEN   *(with the "Stroke" book in his hand)* They say there are four
angry, horrible things that you may feel:
resentment
undifferentiated rage
humiliation
and
guilt.

> *VOICES in the soundscape.*

ZOE   It's the mood swings that get to you – from tears to laughter.

BEN   Whose? His or hers?

ZOE   Or yours?

> *They make eye contact and share a look from opposite sides of the stage. Lights shift down on ZOE. BEN starts reading again from the "Stroke" book, while "Hinterland Who's Who" comes in underneath.*

BEN   "Don't relegate him to the sidelines and leave him with only television and radio to occupy himself. Encourage him to develop a hobby. Spend time with him. Perhaps he will enjoy playing checkers, chess or bridge."

> *Lights shift.*

Scene Nineteen

> *BEN and ZOE enter the living/dining room where the GENERAL is reading.*

ZOE   Dad, you feel like having a game of crib?

GENERAL   What are you talking about?

ZOE   You want to play cards?

GENERAL   NO!!!

ZOE   Guess not.

BEN   Well, let's do something.

ZOE   Yeah, what?

> *Pause.*

Do you remember when we actually used to sometimes have fun together?

BEN   Yeah – like when we used to rent that cottage up at Swallow Lake?

LILITH   *(from the kitchen)* I loved that cottage.

GENERAL   All you ever did was complain about the spiders.

LILITH   But, I loved it.

BEN   Yeah, that was great – remember when you used to get up and recite that poem about the horse? What was that? "The horse has…" What was it?

ZOE   I don't remember that.

LILITH   *(dancing into the room)* Zoey used to think she was really clever. She was so cute. She'd say: "Want to hear a dirty joke? A white horse fell in the mud."

BEN   I never got the joke.

GENERAL   I taught her that.

LILITH   She used to laugh so hard every time she told it, that she always wet herself.

> *She takes a snap of ZOE.*

ZOE   I don't remember that.

BEN   Didn't we always play charades when we were up there?

ZOE   Yeah – we did! I used to be really good at that.

GENERAL   So did I.

LILITH   I was never any good at that game.

BEN   Let's play charades!!!

ZOE   Seriously?

BEN   Why not? What do you think, Mom?

LILITH   *(dancing faster)* Oh, I don't know… Donald won't—

GENERAL   I want to play charades.

> *He puts on his other glasses.*

BEN   Okay. Zoe – you go first.

ZOE   Don't we have to write things down and put them in a hat, pick teams and all that?

BEN   No – just make it up. You go first.

ZOE   Okay. Ummmmm. Okay. Okay. I've got one.

> *She does the gestures to indicate a movie.*

GENERAL   A movie!!!

ZOE   Yes! Okay. Okay.

> *Holding up three fingers.*

BEN   Three words.

ZOE   Okay. *(holding up one finger)*

LILITH   First word.

> *ZOE holds thumb and finger together to indicate short word.*

A?

> *ZOE shakes her head.*

BEN   An?

> *ZOE shakes her head.*

GENERAL   The!!!

> *He slams his hand on the table and accidentally knocks the book on the floor.*

ZOE   Right!

> *Holding up two fingers.*

LILITH   Donald! Calm down.

> *She bends to pick up the book, takes a picture of it and puts it on the table – he pushes it out of his way.*

BEN   Second word!

> *ZOE holds up one finger.*

First syllable.

> *ZOE shakes her head.*

One syllable?

> *Nodding her head, ZOE spreads her arms out wide.*

GENERAL   Big!

> *ZOE shakes her head.*

BEN   Large!

> *ZOE shakes her head.*

LILITH   Huge.

> *ZOE shakes her head.*

GENERAL   Great!

ZOE   Yes! *(holds up three fingers)*

BEN   Third word.

GENERAL   "The Great Escape"!!!

ZOE   Yes!

BEN   Good going, Dad. How did you get that so fast?

GENERAL   That's my favourite movie.

> *He starts to hum the music from the movie – "Da Dum, Da Da Da Dum Dum…" and ZOE joins in. LILITH snaps a photo – flash.*

BEN   *(to ZOE)* Did you know that?

ZOE   Well, yeah.

> *ZOE stops singing but the GENERAL keeps singing.*

BEN   Cheater!

ZOE   I'm not!!!

GENERAL   My turn!

LILITH   Donald, are you sure you want to /

GENERAL   It's my turn.

> *He does the gesture to indicate a song, making a loud sound with it.*

LILITH   Sssshhh. It's charades.

BEN   Song!

ZOE   How many words?

GENERAL   *(slowly counting in his head first, then out loud, using his right hand)* One, two, three, four, five, six.

> *He lifts his left hand with his right, holding up his hand with five fingers showing—even though some of them are bent almost closed—along with his pinky finger on his right hand.*

LILITH   Oh, Donald, that's too /

ZOE   Six words. Okay.

BEN   First word.

GENERAL   No.

> *He holds his right hand over his left, holding all of his fingers together.*

LILITH   What are you doing? What's wrong?

ZOE   I don't get it?

BEN   Do you mean that you're going to do them all at once?

GENERAL   Together.

> *He drops his hands in his lap and looks around at stuff on the table, while everybody watches him. LILITH and ZOE exchange a glance.*

LILITH   *(starting to dance faster)* Donald?…

GENERAL   Just a minute!

> *He picks up his cigarette package, holds it over his head and then drops it on his head. They all freeze and stare at him and then exchange glances – then ZOE bends over to pick up the cigarettes and put them back on the table.*

LILITH   Donald, are you all right?

> *The GENERAL picks up the cigarettes and just looks at them.*

ZOE   Dad…

> *He drops the cigarettes on his head again.*

LILITH   Donald, let me help…

> *She starts to try to help him somehow.*

GENERAL   Leave me alone.

> *LILITH picks up dancing speed as she backs away from him.*

BEN   *(picking up the cigarettes and giving them to the GENERAL)* It's a song!!!

ZOE   What?

> *The GENERAL drops the cigarettes on his head again. LILITH dances faster.*

BEN   It's a song. What is it? Falling?

> *He picks up the cigarettes and hands them to him.*

ZOE   "Falling in Love Again"?

GENERAL   No.

> *He drops them on his head again.*

BEN   "Please Help Me I'm Falling"?

> *Picking them up and putting them on the table.*

GENERAL   NO!!!

> *He holds his good hand over his head and makes little motions with his fingers.*

LILITH   Donald, what are you doing?

GENERAL   Look!!!

> *He does the motion with his hand again.*

l to r: Ryan Rogerson, Gay Hauser, John Dartt and Krista Laveck
Photo by Charlie Rhindress

ZOE   What is that? What are you doing? Dancing? Flicking? Snowing?

BEN   Raining? Rain?

GENERAL   Yes!!!

> *He stops doing the rain thing and picks up the cigarettes and drops them on his head again.*

BEN   "Raindrops Keep Falling On My Head"!!!

GENERAL   Yes!!!

ZOE   You're kidding! *(to BEN)* How did you get that?

BEN   It was obvious.

> *He starts to sing "Raindrops Keep Falling On My Head."*

ZOE   It was not.

GENERAL   I told you I was good at charades. *(pause)* Gimme my cigarettes.

> *LILITH picks up the cigarettes and dances over to the table and starts to re-arrange everything on the table, moving his glasses, book, etc.*

What are you doing? What are you doing?

LILITH I just thought I'd tidy up a /

GENERAL Leave it alone. Leave ME alone.

BEN Dad, let's play again.

ZOE Yeah, Ben, it's your turn.

GENERAL What time is it? Where's the remote?

BEN Dad…

LILITH Donald…

> *He has the remote and turns on the TV—sound blasts— the theme from "Happy Days." He is immediatelly focused on the TV.*

GENERAL Make me a coffee, will you?

> *LILITH looks at ZOE and BEN and then dances off.*

ZOE Well, that was fun. Now, what do you want to do?

> *BEN glares at her and exits – following LILITH into the kitchen. ZOE stays in the living/dining room. She watches/hears the following scene and watches the GENERAL watching TV.*

Scene Twenty

> *Lights up in the kitchen where BEN is standing and LILITH is quietly dancing around, holding a carton of milk.*

BEN I hate him.

> *LILITH stops dancing.*

I don't care if he is crippled now and I should feel sorry for him. I don't. I hate him!!

LILITH   *(staring at BEN in disbelief)* But, why?

BEN   Because… I just hate him. *(He turns away.)*

> Pause. LILITH slowly starts dancing again, humming
> quietly, slowly building in tempo.

(turning and directing this straight at LILITH) I just HATE him!
(He exits.)

> LILITH drops the milk. She stops dead. Stares at the
> spilt milk and bursts into tears and sobs and sobs.
> Lights shift.

> BEN in his room, once again reading from the "Stroke"
> book, while "Hinterland's Who's Who" plays
> underneath – increasing in volume.

"But we need not look only to the future for hope and help for
the stroke patient. Every stroke patient has a brighter outlook
because of what can be done now—today—by medical
science, by the family and by the patient himself."

GENERAL   Lilith! Where's my coffee?

> BEN throws the book at the wall as the "Hinterland"
> theme heightens and builds to a crescendo, then cuts
> out.

GENERAL & ZOE   *(his pre-stroke voice and her voice together, over)*
It would be good to know why things happened the way they
did, don't you think?

> The GENERAL and ZOE exchange a look.

Scene Twenty-One

> Lights and sound and smoke transition through a series
> of TV selections which warp as they go along, indicating
> a passage of considerable time.
> The GENERAL is sitting at the table in the wheelchair –
> more pieces of his uniform gone. He's wearing his
> glasses and leaning over reading a book with a
> magnifying glass. There's a lit cigarette in the ashtray

and the room is very smoky. There is a lot of stuff on the table: TV remote control, ashtray, cigarettes, lighter, lamp, another pair of glasses, books, watch, magazines, TV guide, etc.

ZOE is in the kitchen, reading a magazine.

BEN is in his room, juggling. As the scene progresses, he actively listens, before moving into the living/dining room.

The GENERAL takes a drag off of the cigarette then slowly puts it out. He puts a bookmark in the book, closes it, puts it aside, picks up the watch – looks at the time and puts it down, then takes off his glasses, puts them on the table and picks up and puts on his other glasses.

GENERAL   *(calling out to whoever will answer)* What time's your mother getting home?

ZOE   What?

GENERAL   What time's your mother getting home?

ZOE   *(going into living/dining room)* I don't know for sure – probably about five o'clock or so. Depends on the traffic I guess – what time she gets away.

GENERAL   She's driving?

ZOE   Yes. You knew that. She asked you if she could take the car.

GENERAL   Oh. What time is it now?

ZOE   About eight-thirty, I think

GENERAL   What?

ZOE   About eight-thirty.

GENERAL   What do you mean?

ZOE   What?

GENERAL   What are you TALKING ABOUT?

ZOE   What do you mean?

GENERAL   Where's your mother?

ZOE   What?

GENERAL   Where's your mother?

ZOE   I don't know what you're... she's in Hamilton—visiting her cousin—you know that.

GENERAL   Don't LIE to me. Everybody *lies* to me. She's a *liar!*

ZOE   What're you talking about? Calm down. What's the matter?

GENERAL   What's she doing in Hamilton? She said she was going to see Betty Sampson.

ZOE   No, Dad. She was thinking of visiting Betty, or of going there first and then on to Hamilton, but she decided only to go to Hamilton, so she wouldn't have to drive so much.

GENERAL   What are you talking about?

ZOE   I don't know what you mean. Why are you so upset?

          BEN enters.

BEN   What's all the yelling about? You two having a fight? You know I hate to miss a good fight.

ZOE   We're not fighting.

GENERAL   Where's your mother?

BEN   In Hamilton, visiting Uncle John.

GENERAL   *Christ!*

BEN   Isn't she?

GENERAL   Nobody tells me *anything!*

BEN   What?

GENERAL   When's she getting home?

BEN   Tomorrow.

GENERAL *Tomorrow??*

BEN Yeah… Monday? That's tomorrow, isn't it?

GENERAL You said she'd be home at five-thirty!

ZOE Five-thirty—tomorrow—depending on when she gets away.

GENERAL She said she'd be home today!!

ZOE No, Dad, tomorrow.

GENERAL What are you talking about? She said she'd be home today!

ZOE No, Dad.

BEN I don't think so.

GENERAL She lied to me! She's always lying! She's gone to that cousin of hers!

ZOE Dad, you knew that.

GENERAL Her cousin's *crazy!!* He's a stupid bastard!

ZOE Yeah.

BEN So?

GENERAL She never tells me *anything.* She never listens to me! Nobody listens to me! She listens to her cousin. That *bastard* John!

ZOE No she doesn't.

BEN Not always.

GENERAL Always. ALWAYS. She said she'd be home today.

ZOE No.

GENERAL Yes she DID. She lied to me. She lied. Get me the phone!

ZOE *(almost starts to get the phone but stops)* What for?

GENERAL Get me the phone!

BEN   Why do you want the phone?

GENERAL   I'm gonna call her and tell her to get HOME!

ZOE   But, Dad, if she's still there, she can't…

GENERAL   Get me the phone!

> *Pause.*

ZOE   No.

> *Pause.*

GENERAL   She said she'd be home tonight!

ZOE   No.

GENERAL   SHE DID! She did!

ZOE   Well shit – maybe she did. I don't know.

BEN   She's coming tomorrow.

ZOE   I'm mixed up, I don't know anymore.

GENERAL   Give me the phone!

ZOE   You're not gonna call her.

> *He starts trying to get to the phone himself, can't really move the chair, gets even more frustrated and starts smashing things on the table and pushing/throwing them.*

Stop it.

BEN   Cut it out. What's wrong with just us being here?

ZOE   Don't you trust us?

GENERAL   I don't trust her. I don't trust that cousin of hers. I never did. He's always scheming. He always lies. He never minds his own business. I should've killed him when I had the chance – making me scare the kid like that. I had to… CHRIST!!! Your mother believed him! She always believes HIM!!!

ZOE   Not always, Dad.

GENERAL   ALWAYS. Give me the phone. I'll tell her! I'll kill her!

ZOE   You're not going to call and upset her like that. If she's upset she won't be able to drive and she'll WRECK YOUR CAR. Besides if you call now you'll just give that *bastard cousin, uncle John,* an excuse to start.

GENERAL   He doesn't need an excuse.

BEN   True.

GENERAL   She lied to me.

ZOE   I don't think she did. It just got mixed up.

GENERAL   I'm not mixed up!

BEN   Well, I sure am.

ZOE   So am I. What's the problem? Why can't she go away for a few days? Can't she even get a break?

GENERAL   I never get a break.

> *Pause. Silence as they all take this one in.*

BEN   What are you so worried about?

ZOE   Are you worried about her driving?

GENERAL   She won't come back.

ZOE   What?

GENERAL   That COUSIN OF HERS will talk her into not COMING BACK.

ZOE   That's crazy.

GENERAL   I'm not CRAZY. She gets with that cousin of hers and she's so stupid she can't even think for herself.

ZOE   That's not true.

GENERAL   *It is.* She's an idiot.

ZOE   She just went away for a few days.

GENERAL   She won't come back!

ZOE   She will.

BEN   *(to ZOE)* Won't she?

ZOE   She wouldn't do that to us – would she?

GENERAL   Give me the *phone! (pause)* I'll kill her!

> *While the GENERAL starts bashing stuff around again, bangs the table, gets hold of the TV remote and goes to throw it at the TV, ZOE is muttering: "Stop it. Stop it," and is backing out of room; she moves back toward the kitchen – as he goes to throw the remote.*

BEN   PUT THAT DOWN!

> *GENERAL stops dead.*

GENERAL   Put it down?! I won't. I'm gonna throw it.

BEN   You'll break the TV!

GENERAL   So what? I'm gonna break it.

BEN   NO. You're not.

l to r: Ryan Rogerson and John Dartt
Photo by Charlie Rhindress

> *Stops him dead again.*

GENERAL Why not?

BEN Because I'm the only one in this bloody family who's working and I'll have to buy a new one!

> *Silence. The GENERAL doesn't know whether to laugh or cry – he sputters then puts the remote down. After a pause he starts to try to find a cigarette, fumbles around.*

You want a cigarette?

GENERAL Yes.

> *BEN gets the smokes and lighter and ashtray for him. He lights up and then just sits there. Again, the room becomes very smoky. BEN sits down across from him. Silence. The GENERAL reaches for his book – can't reach it.*

BEN What do you want? Your book?

GENERAL I guess so.

> *BEN gets the book for him from where it fell.*

Where are my reading glasses?

BEN How should I know? Which way did you throw them?

> *GENERAL doesn't know whether to laugh or cry. He sputters. BEN laughs, then the GENERAL sort of laughs. BEN finds his glasses for him and he goes through the routine of changing glasses and opening the book. BEN sits down across the table from the GENERAL and watches for a moment – then starts to read a magazine and squeeze the GENERAL's rubber exercise ball, that he picked up off the floor.*

ZOE *(in the kitchen on the phone, speaking quietly)* Hello – Uncle John? Hi. *(pause)* No. Everything's fine. How are you? Is Mom there? *(pause)* No. Everything's fine. Can I talk to my mother? *(pause)* Please? *(pause)* Listen, this is none of your business. *(pause)* Yeah? *(pause)* Really? Well, listen, John – he's my father, okay? Maybe you could keep your opinion to yourself on that, okay? *(pause)* So, could you please let me talk to my goddamned mother? Now? Thank you. *(pause)* Scheming, lying bastard.

LILITH   *(appearing behind a scrim, dancing)* What's wrong?

ZOE   Hi. *(struggling to be calm)* How are you?

LILITH   Has something happened?

ZOE   No – nothing's wrong. You having a good time?

LILITH   Oh. *(She starts to dance faster.)* Yes, sure, fine.

ZOE   What're you doing?

LILITH   Oh – we went to the fall fair.

ZOE   That's nice. Was it good?

LILITH   Um, yes, it's always nice.

ZOE   How's Aunt Sarah?

LILITH   Oh, you know…

ZOE   Yeah – just like always. I just called to see /

LILITH   Is he upset?

ZOE   No.

LILITH   Is something wrong?

ZOE   He's just a little confused. He thought you were coming home today.

LILITH   Why did he think that? I told him I'd be back tomorrow.

ZOE   I don't know. *I knew* it was tomorrow. You are coming home?

LILITH   Of course, I'm /

ZOE   He got me a little confused. I just thought if I called, it might calm him down – and keep him from trying to call.

LILITH   Maybe I'd better start back right now.

ZOE   No – don't do that. Everything's fine.

LILITH   I'm going to leave right now.

ZOE   No. *Don't do that!* I'm sorry, I shouldn't have called. When are you leaving? Tomorrow – what time are you planning to leave tomorrow?

LILITH   I was planning to try to get away around noon.

ZOE   So – you should be here by about three then?

LILITH   At the latest.

ZOE   Yeah – I told him five-thirty, so three would be great. Yeah.

LILITH   I can leave earlier if you…

ZOE   No, no. It's okay. It's kind of…. See ya tomorrow. Drive carefully. 'Night.

>   *She hangs up. Lights out on LILITH.*

>   *The GENERAL goes through the routine of closing his book and changing his glasses and starts to look for his watch.*

GENERAL   What time is it?

BEN   What?

GENERAL   What TIME is it?

BEN   I don't know. Where's your watch?

GENERAL   I DON'T KNOW!

BEN   Which way did you throw IT?

GENERAL   SHUT UP.

BEN   Why don't you shut up?

GENERAL   QUIT AGGRAVATING ME!

BEN   Sorry.

GENERAL   It doesn't work anyway.

BEN   What?

GENERAL   It's no good anyway. I can't read it. I told her I couldn't see it. I *told* her. She wouldn't listen. She *never* listens.

BEN   Yeah.

ZOE   *(in the kitchen)* Now what? *(She gets up and goes into the other room.)* What's wrong now?

GENERAL   Don't you START. You're just like your MOTHER.

> *The VOICES come in intensely in the soundscape –*
> *ZOE reacts.*

ZOE   Oh for Christ's sake I AM NOT!!

GENERAL   Nothing's ever good enough for her. *Nothing.*

ZOE   What are you talking about now?

GENERAL   Nothing's good enough for her except her cousin, John! Nothing I ever give her is good enough.

ZOE   That's not true.

GENERAL   It is. It is. I bought *her* a watch. She never wears it. She wears that cheap one her cousin gave her.

ZOE   What?

GENERAL   Ben and me picked it out of the catalogue – the one she said she wanted and Ben went and got it for me and she never wears it.

ZOE   Is that true?

BEN   Uh huh.

GENERAL   I'm telling you!

ZOE   JESUS CHRIST!

> *The VOICES kick in.*
> *ZOE reaches across the table and takes and lights one of his cigarettes. The room fills with smoke as she inhales deeply – the deep inhalation is echoed in the soundscape and goes on and on and on and on and then the VOICES go "AAAAAAHHHHHHH" as they did*

> *earlier. Silence – it is a long moment. They all just sit there until the GENERAL picks up his watch and looks at it.*

GENERAL   What time is it?

> *ZOE and BEN look at him and then at each other.*

I wish to God somebody'd give me a watch. I can't see the numbers on this. I keep telling her! I can't see this.

> *He throws the watch across the room, nobody reacts. Nobody moves. Silence. Another long moment. Eventually, the GENERAL gets his book and goes through the routine with it and his glasses and starts to read. ZOE slowly moves back to the kitchen, where she puts the cigarette out. Lights start to fade on the GENERAL, shifting to the kitchen. BEN comes into the kitchen and sits.*

BEN   What's the hardest part of a vegetable to eat?

ZOE   I don't know, what?

> *Pause.*

BEN   The wheelchair.

> *Pause – it's a disgusting thing to say.*

ZOE   That's disgusting!

BEN   Yeah. It's disgusting all right.

> *They look at each other and then start to laugh. The laughter goes on and on and echoes and echoes madly and loudly in the soundscape as ZOE and BEN cry in the kitchen.*

GENERAL   *(from the other room)* What's going on? What are you laughing at? STOP AGGRAVATING ME!!!

> *Lights and sound shift.*

Scene Twenty-Two

ZOE   *(Entering the living/dining room, carrying a photo in a frame, she goes over to stand next to the GENERAL – on his right side.)* I always liked this picture of you.

GENERAL   I always looked good in pictures.

ZOE   Excuse me!

GENERAL   I'm photogenic. I always looked good. That's why your mother fell for me in the first place.

ZOE   'Cause you were so handsome?

GENERAL   Must've been. She doesn't seem to like anything else about me.

>   *Pause.*

ZOE   Dad, can I ask you something?

GENERAL   WHAT?

ZOE   Don't yell at me!!

>   *Pause.*

GENERAL   Okay.

ZOE   Why do you hate Uncle John so much?

GENERAL   'Cause he's a lazy *prick! (A look is exchanged between them, as in: "don't yell at me.")* And a drunk.

ZOE   But what happened to make you hate him so much?

GENERAL   Lots of things. *(pause)* He was always bumming off us. *(pause)* One time – he was living here, out of work, drinking all day. Sarah had kicked him out. I was supporting everybody. One night he passed out in the chair and dropped a cigarette and set the chair on fire. Nearly burned the house down.

ZOE   You're kidding. When was this?

GENERAL   Ben was about three.

ZOE   Why don't I remember any of this? Where was I when all this was going on?

GENERAL   Probably in your room, playing with your dolls – that's where you usually were.

ZOE   Oh.

VOICES.

GENERAL   Ben liked John. They used to sit around and read comic books together all day. Coupla weeks after the fire, I came home from work and caught Ben lighting matches and throwing them at the couch to see if he could start a fire too.

ZOE   What did you do?

GENERAL   I took a match and lit it and blew it out and held it to his arm and burnt him!

ZOE   What?

GENERAL   How else was he gonna understand? It's dangerous to play with matches!

ZOE   Wow!

GENERAL   So John takes a swing at me and tells me I'm a lousy father.

ZOE   Oh.

GENERAL   So, I belted him and threw him out and I told him, "You're not his father. I am." And Ben said:

BEN   *(his three-year-old voice)* "I wish Uncle John was my daddy."

ZOE   Oh.

GENERAL   Your mother never forgave me.

LILITH   *(her voice)* What kind of a father burns his own child?

GENERAL   Neither did Ben. I might as well have killed the scheming bastard. I never did understand why your mother liked John so much, though.

ZOE   Me neither.

GENERAL   Felt responsible for him I guess, like a younger brother.

ZOE   I guess.

GENERAL   Like you and Ben.

> *VOICES.*

ZOE   ...Oh.

GENERAL   Ben wishes John was his father instead of me.

ZOE   I don't think so.

GENERAL   Maybe I wasn't very good at being a father. Ran out of time, I guess.

> *Pause.*

ZOE   Well, speaking of time, Dad, I have to go back home tomorrow.

GENERAL   Oh.

ZOE   So, I bought you a going away present.

GENERAL   I'm not going away!!!

ZOE   No, I am. So I bought you a present.

GENERAL   Oh. What?

> *She hands him a box. He changes his glasses and tries to open the box. He can't so he shoves it toward her. She opens it – it's a watch with a big face and big oversized numbers. She hands it to him.*

ZOE   Can you see the numbers?

> *The GENERAL nods.*

(*picking up the box*) Guess I'll just put this away in your room, okay?

> *As ZOE exits, he stares at the watch.*

GENERAL   Thanks.

He watches her leave. Then he picks up the remote and turns on the TV – "The Rockford Files" theme blares. Lights down on GENERAL.

Scene Twenty-Three

ZOE is at her place, writing on the walls, while talking on the phone to BEN who is sitting on his futon, juggling.

ZOE   He doesn't seem to be able to hide his feelings anymore.

BEN   No kidding.

ZOE   Well, no, but I mean, it's like a part of him that he'd always kept hidden has been – revealed. A part of him that I – that we – might never have gotten to see – to know. Some of it's nice.

BEN   Most of it isn't.

ZOE   Yeah, but some of it's surprising, eh? Like who knew? The level of his inhibitions has changed or something – as if his protective armour was damaged. It's almost as if that's the one good thing that has happened – we've gotten a chance to know him differently.

BEN   Yeah, sure. Whatever you say.

The VOICES are back.

ZOE   Well, I'm grateful for that in some odd way. In a strange way, it's been a kind of a gift.

BEN   Some gift!

Lights shift.

Scene Twenty-Four

The GENERAL is peacefully asleep in the wheelchair at the table in the living/dining room. He wakes up very calmly and gently, smiling – a satisfied sigh. His eyes open. He looks around awkwardly, which shocks him, he becomes more and more disoriented and frightened. He tries to move, discovers he is even more paralyzed from a new stroke. He fumbles and panics.

GENERAL   *(screams)* CHRIST! *(pause)* ZOE!

> *Pause. He fumbles around some more and struggles, yells again:*

LILITH!!! LILITH!!!

> *Lights and sound shift.*

Scene Twenty-Five

> *In the darkness, we hear ZOE's phone ringing several times. Lights up on her, sleeping. She wakes up and doesn't know where she is at first. She freezes as, after several rings, the answering machine picks up and then we hear BEN's voice:*

BEN   Zoe, it's Ben. It's three in the morning here. The hospital just called. The General is pretty bad. We're on our way over there now. *(pause, then his voice breaks slightly – very briefly)* It looks like this may be it. We'll call. We'll call from the hospital. *(pause)* We'll call later.

> *The answering machine does that really irritating noise for a while, then stops as the VOICES drift in and out with ZOE as she sits frozen in bed with the phone in her lap. The lights shift but are still on ZOE throughout the next scene.*

Scene Twenty-Six

> *The hospital – the GENERAL in bed. Sounds: moans, squeals, voices – bedlam. The soundscape plays in full force in the hospital—with various background sounds—hospital ambience. LILITH and BEN are there.*

LILITH   Oh. The car. We have to go move the car – the meter…

BEN   I'll stay here – you go ahead.

LILITH dances off.

GENERAL   *(coming to)* I'm hearing the voices again.

BEN   What voices? What are they saying?

GENERAL   I DON'T KNOW!!! I'm trying to block them out. *(starts to sing)* "Toreador don't spit on the floor. Use the cuspidor…"

OLD GUY   *(his voice from the bed across from the GENERAL)* He kept us up all night. He never stops complaining. He screamed all night.

BEN   He's my father.

OLD GUY   He was yelling so loud he was rattling the windows. He shouldn't be here.

BEN   Where should he be?

LILITH   *(dancing back into the room)* They moved him last night – down the hall. Put him in a room by himself. It was so small, the bed didn't fit. They finally put him on Halidol – and brought him back here.

OLD GUY   They should have left him in there – he's crazy.

BEN   Hey!

GENERAL   Asshole!

LILITH   They put him in this little tiny room.

OLD GUY   He's crazy!

BEN   Mister, why don't you fuck off! *(turns to LILITH)* Sorry, Mum.

GENERAL   Get away. Get away. Get away. I'm not gonna die in…. I'm not gonna die in… I'm not gonna die in…. Get it out. Take it out…. Take it out. I need a, I need a. I need a… I need a… to hit him. Lily! Lily! LILITH!

LILITH   For God's sake, I'm going to find a nurse.

She walks off.

BEN   Dad, Dad, it's okay.

OLD GUY   Make him shut up.

BEN   You shut up.

GENERAL   Dad, don't hit her. OWOWOWOWOWOWOWOW. You're pulling my hair. I had… I had to… I had to hit him. Tell your ma, I had to do it.

BEN   Who, Dad? Who did you have to hit?

GENERAL   The kid, the kid. I scared the kid! John, you lying, scheming bastard! Mind your own business. Get out. Get out. Get out of my house. Leave my wife and kid alone. I didn't mean… I didn't mean… I had to… CHRIST!!!

> *BEN stares at him, unable to speak.*

(singing) …don't spit on the floor…
Lily! Don't leave with him!!!

> *He tries to whistle and can't, then starts to suck in air as if he's smoking, then starts to sing an old cigarette ad.*

"…da da da da.… A true smoker's treasure
…la… la la la.… The brand for sophisticates…"

> *He sucks in air again.*

Mmmmmmmmmm. Good."

BEN   You're dreamin', eh?

GENERAL   Oh, yeah.

BEN   Do you know where you are?

GENERAL   "The smoothest cigarette that you've tasted yet. That's why the move today is to.… La… la… la… la…"

> *He tries to whistle.*

BEN   Dad!

GENERAL   Yes, damn you.

> *Pause.*

I didn't mean to. I didn't mean to. Didn't mean to. He had it comin'. One of you.… One of you.… Ooooh. Yahoooo.

OLD GUY   Shut up, you crazy bastard.

BEN   You shut up.

GENERAL   I have to go to the bathroom.

BEN   You want to go to the bathroom?

GENERAL   Well. I think I'd better so I won't have to get up in the night. Yoohoo. Youoooooooooooooo.

BEN   I'm going to get Mum. Hang on, okay?

> *He exits. There is a momentary quiet in the room.*

GENERAL   I'm dyin'.

OLD GUY   Crazy bastard.

> *GENERAL blows a raspberry at the OLD GUY in the other bed, then dies.*
> *Silence. ZOE sitting bolt upright in her bed.*

ZOE   Dad?

> *She blows a raspberry. The sound amplifies and echoes loudly through the soundscape.*
> *Lights down on the hospital.*

Scene Twenty-Seven

> *Lights shift back to ZOE sitting frozen with the phone in her lap, at her place. The phone rings. She grabs it on the first ring. (In this scene neither of them gives into the emotion, only break for either of them comes where specifically indicated and is very brief and tightly controlled.)*

ZOE   Hello?

BEN   It's Ben.

ZOE   Where are you?

BEN   We're at the house.

> *Pause.*

BEN   He died at three-thirty.

ZOE   Uh huh. *(on an intake of breath)*

> *VOICES.*

BEN   When nobody was there.

> *VOICES.*

ZOE   Are you okay?

BEN   *(stifling a sob – quickly controlling it)* Yeah. Are you?

ZOE   I ran out of cigarettes.

> *She starts to cry. BEN doesn't speak, just breathes heavily into the phone. Long pause with VOICES in.*

(no longer crying) I'll, I'll… the store's open now, I'll go get some smokes. Then I'll call the… I'll call Air Canada. I'll get a flight. I'll call back.

BEN   Okay. Do you know when?

ZOE   Probably… have to be tomorrow. I don't know, maybe I can get out tonight. I have to go to work… I have to call work. I have to… I gotta have a smoke. I'll call as soon as I figure it out.

BEN   Okay. We'll be here for awhile.

ZOE   I'll call. You. Okay?

BEN   Yuh.

> *Silence. They both hang up as the VOICES creep in.*

Scene Twenty-Eight

> *Major transition with lights and sound—going back to the same lights and sound as in the original transition from the day of the funeral to the past—as we return to the day of the funeral. ZOE is standing in the GENERAL's bedroom in the Nightshade home, holding the GENERAL's watch. The GENERAL is lying on the*

bed in his Bermuda shorts and Hawaiian shirt as the
lights come up.

ZOE   So, what the hell are you doing here?

GENERAL   Oh. Yeah, I see now. I had to leave.

He sits up and starts to hum "The Limbo." ZOE turns
to look at him and crosses over to sit with him on the
bed. Noises from other parts of the house – the people
from the funeral.

ZOE   I don't know if you're dead or alive. If you're alive, I don't
think they can cope with it. I mean, they'll be all embarrassed
that things aren't the way they're supposed to be and wanting
to go ahead with the plans – deal with all those people, get on
with things.

GENERAL   That's what those whole ten years were like. Like
you all were just waiting for me to go away all the time?

ZOE   …No…

GENERAL   …Like limbo…

He starts to whistle "The Limbo."

ZOE   Ten years. Was it really that long?

The GENERAL nods and keeps whistling.

I'm lonely. I'm really lonely in this family without you.
Nobody else makes any sense. Well, not that you make any
sense either, but.… There's no reason for me to be here
anymore. They're with "company," telling these stories –
they're doing the memory lane bullshit – about everything
and everybody *except* you! *(laughter from the kitchen)* What is
that about?

GENERAL   …Just what people do, I guess.

The lights shift to reveal LILITH and BEN in the
kitchen with the flowers and food. Muffled voices and
laughter from the other room, there's the suggestion of
many other people present in the house.

ZOE   I wish I could just leave.

GENERAL   Why don't you?

ZOE   God only knows.

GENERAL   I know what you mean.

ZOE   There's no reason to stay.

GENERAL   Nope.

ZOE   Everything's over. I really need to get back to work.
There's no reason for me to be here anymore. I'm gonna call
the airport. I paid full fare and they're gonna give me some of
it back anyway, so it can't cost anything to change it.

GENERAL   I think I paid full fare too.

ZOE   Well, you sure didn't exactly go gently into…

GENERAL   Yeah, yeah, yeah…

> *He elbows her and starts to hum "The Limbo" again,
> then elbows her again to make her hum "The Limbo"
> along with him.*

> *In the kitchen:*

LILITH   Dorothy Shephard asked me if I thought I could
volunteer for Meals on Wheels now that I would have more
spare time. She says they need drivers. And Alice asked me if
I thought I could volunteer at the hospital now and Marion
wants me to start canvassing with her for Save the Children
and Sal wants me to volunteer at the stroke patients' recovery
group every Thursday. Was the house clean enough? I tried
and tried to get the stains out of the carpet. That damned
carpet. I always hated that damned thing. What good is
a beige carpet? Every single thing that's spilled on it shows
up forever, but he had to buy that one – his pal could get it
wholesale so whatever I wanted to do in terms of decorating
didn't matter. Everything had to match that damned carpet
that just got dirtier and dirtier every year and the drapes and
all the furniture, everything just got dingier and dingier as
he sat there twenty-four hours a day smoking cigarette after
cigarette – he went through two packs a day, just sat there for
ten years smoking. The whole house stinks. The whole house

is stained yellow. What did people think? Nicotine stains and smoke trapped everywhere. Did the funeral look cheap? Do you think they thought I was cheap? Do you think I didn't.... Did they think the service was too Anglican? But what else could I do – he wouldn't go to church. He wouldn't do anything. I just went back to church to make sure he could get buried, but he never would talk to the minister when he came to the house – what could the minister talk about? He never even got to know him. He only met him after.... He offered to give him communion when he came to the house but he wouldn't do it. He said he was no damned Catholic and nobody was going to give him the last rites.... Do you think everything was all right? If only he hadn't... if only we'd... why didn't we ever... why couldn't he... why...

She dances herself offstage.

BEN *(yelling off to ZOE)* Zoe, you know what I read in the paper today – well, I know you're searching for something on the cosmic level here, and I think I have it, this is it—overnight, three days ago—the night he died – Mars and Saturn formed a rare merger.

GENERAL What bull. I wonder when Ben learned to spout the bull like that. Like your mother's family – a lot like your Uncle John.

BEN The general description for Capricorn—his sign—was victory in a personal dispute. I don't know for sure what that means, but I thought you'd find it interesting. Zoe?

> *An instrumental version of "The Limbo" starts to play as LILITH dances across the space to the bedroom door, which she unlocks with a key. She crosses to the bed. ZOE crawls under a blanket and pulls it over her head. LILITH can't see the GENERAL.*

LILITH It was a good turnout. He really was a pillar of the community, you know. They did love him out there and that's very important. He would have enjoyed it better if it had been ten years ago. Imagine the crowd there would have been then. He would have liked a *really* big send off. He used to love those big ostentatious parties – all that show.

*LILITH lifts the blanket and snaps a photo of ZOE
under the blankets. ZOE groans really loudly and
thrashes out at LILITH who sits on the bed. The
GENERAL is whistling "The Limbo" and waving his
hands in front of LILITH's face to get her attention.
LILITH lies down on the bed with ZOE, though her legs
are still in motion—almost twitching—she can't quite
stop dancing.*

GENERAL   I never could communicate with that woman. Never
really could talk to Ben either. *(pause)* I guess I let him down.

ZOE   How?

GENERAL   Well, Zoe, I guess you'll just have to ask him about
that.

LILITH   I was so scared. *(She lies still, not even twitching.)* I didn't
know what to do anymore. I couldn't do it anymore. I'm worn
out. My legs are tired. And there was nowhere for him to go.
Nowhere in the world. No one would take him.

ZOE   Why?

LILITH   He smoked. It's all he had. TV and cigarettes and large
print books – that was his whole life and no one would take
him. Even if we had sold the house to pay for a nursing home
– no one would take him. *(pause)* I'm so tired.

ZOE   Why did he hate Uncle John so much?

LILITH   What? What does that matter now? *(Her legs start to
move again.)*

ZOE   What's the big secret?

LILITH   Why does it have to be a big secret? Maybe it's none of
your business.

She gets up and is dancing again.

ZOE   Because big secrets lurk around like ghosts affecting
everything that happens! They're bound to come out
sometime. They need to come out at some point.

LILITH   No, they don't!

ZOE   What's Ben's problem with Dad?

LILITH   He doesn't have a problem with Dad.

ZOE   What?

LILITH   It doesn't matter. We don't need to talk about that.

ZOE   Was it because Dad burnt him?

LILITH   What?

ZOE   Ben said that in the hospital Dad said, "I scared the kid." What was that all about?

LILITH   Nothing. It was all about nothing. Why can't you ever just leave things alone?

GENERAL   Lilith! Where's my hat? I'm in a hurry.

ZOE   Mom, where's Dad's hat?

LILITH   What?

GENERAL   What have you done with my hat?

ZOE   What have you done with Dad's hat?

LILITH   I… nothing… I was going to give it to John.

ZOE & GENERAL   John!!! Get it back! Get it back!

LILITH   I didn't give it to him yet. I was just thinking about…

ZOE & GENERAL   Get it back from that bastard!

LILITH jumps and dances off.

GENERAL   You'd think she could at least wait a few days before she starts giving my stuff away. Hasn't she ever heard of a suitable period of mourning?

ZOE   *(She puts the GENERAL's big watch on as she talks to him.)* We can't mourn 'cause there's no tears left. They've been frozen for too long. You can't mourn someone who isn't dead. It's un-mourning. Un-mourning – and waste. And being left – frozen. But what difference does it make? Usually when someone dies, everybody practically sanctifies them in their eulogies afterwards. It's sickening. When someone who's been in limbo for ten years dies, we just sweep them under the rug.

> *The VOICES kick into the soundscape. ZOE lights a cigarette – smoke fills the room and the VOICES fade.*

GENERAL *(pointing to his watch on ZOE's wrist)* You keep that.

> *Pause. LILITH dances back in, carrying the hat.*

LILITH Zoey, you keep this.

> *She gives the hat to ZOE and starts to dance away.*

ZOE Nice watch, Mom.

LILITH *(stopped in her tracks – she dances on the spot)* Oh! Yes, isn't it beautiful? I've always loved this watch.

ZOE Where'd you get it? Uncle John give you that?

LILITH What? No. Your father gave me this watch. He and Ben picked it out for me.

ZOE I've never seen you wear it before.

LILITH This is my good watch. I always saved it to wear for something special. I wore that cheap one that Uncle John gave me for everyday.

ZOE Haven't you ever worn this one before?

LILITH *(Pause. She stops dancing.)* I guess we didn't go anywhere special for a long time.

> *She deflates as if the air has gone out of her and she shuffles/dances out of the room while the GENERAL and ZOE watch her.*

ZOE We all ran out of time, I guess.

> *BEN appears at the door to the bedroom.*

BEN I miss him too, you know.

ZOE What was your problem with him?

BEN Problem? I don't know what you mean.

ZOE   What he said in the hospital. The whole story about Uncle John. You said you hated him that time…

BEN   I don't remember ever saying that.

ZOE   Ben. He thought he let you down.

BEN   He did – he got sick.

ZOE   What about the whole thing with John?

BEN   What thing?

ZOE   The matches, the fire, the fight.

BEN   Honestly, Zoe, I don't know what you're talking about. Can't you just drop it?

ZOE   I need to talk about him. And nobody will LET ME!

BEN   Zoe, it's just a bit late for you to be trying to figure things out now.

ZOE   What's that supposed to mean?

BEN   Just – it's a bit late to be talking about who let who down. Just… just… leave it alone.

> *He exits.*
> *From offstage we hear LILITH's voice speaking to BEN.*

LILITH   Why can't she ever just leave things alone?

> *A loud crash – the sound of a car slamming into a garage door the full soundscape of whispering VOICES kicks in – the words, at first barely audible, build in volume and clarity, becoming almost distinguishable, saying,* "You're stupid… you're lazy. You're a loser. You've always been a loser. Stupid. Selfish. Messy. Inconsiderate. Self-centred. Irresponsible. Disrespectful. Sloppy. Lazy. Clumsy. Childish. Stupid! Loser. You're a loser. Loser. Loser. Loser. Loser." *It's an endless loop.*

ZOE   Damned weirds! Come *out!* Come out where I can see you.

> *ZOE crawls back under the covers where she lies in a tight knot. The VOICES gain in volume/strength*

again The lights come up as BEN appears (as if in ZOE's head) behind the scrim, he's wearing the top hat and is juggling.

BEN What are the weirds?

ZOE AaaaaHHH!!!

BEN Zoe, what are the weirds?

ZOE They're just – they're just…. Sometimes it's all one big weird. Sometimes… like a… like a… like a big glob of… of… of blyeckk that creeps up on me behind me… slinking along beside me like a stranger… it's stalking me. Sometimes it's like they're hovering overhead and I'm crouching lower and lower to the ground *(She takes on the posture as she describes it.)* like being under a helicopter – ducking the blades and it's coming closer and closer – getting lower and lower. It's a descending weird! And I can't…. I can't get away!

BEN You can't escape?

ZOE Well – I guess no one can escape their own weird.

BEN What does that mean???

Lights come up on LILITH (as if in ZOE's head) behind one of the scrims – dancing and holding a piece of paper in her hand.

LILITH She wrote a poem about them. Want to hear it?

ZOE …What?

BEN …All right…

As LILITH starts to read quickly in a mocking voice, she dances faster, BEN starts to juggle faster, ZOE curls up on top of the bed and the GENERAL starts to do a hand jive.

LILITH "The green eyes on the dresser drawers
are watching me.
I grapple out of the covers.
But don't turn
my back in case the

drawers decide to laugh.
The floor jumps up and trips me.
The rug wraps its twisted tail around my feet.
The door has decided to move and won't let me find it.
It's playing hide and seek so I call out
Ollie Ollie Oxen FREE!
I creep towards the open pit that yawns away below.
Will it be easier to close my eyes and feel the stairs rise up to
     me?
Or
Should I watch to make sure the little elves
who come to mend my clothes for me
aren't sleeping on the landing?
I wouldn't want to smoosh them
cause
I really don't like
to sew."

Pause.

BEN   …Nice.

Camera flashes as LILITH takes a photo.

ZOE   *(cringing in response to the flash)* Mom!

LILITH   Cute poem.

ZOE   Cute???

LILITH   It sounds like a children's story

ZOE   Why? Because of the elves?

BEN   Are the elves the weirds?

ZOE   No. Maybe.

LILITH   Are the elves what you want the weirds to be?

ZOE   What d'you mean?

BEN   They're cute.

LILITH   They're mischievous.

BEN   But not malevolent.

LILITH   They're not mean.

ZOE   I know what malevolent means.

BEN   And you don't want to "smoosh" them.

ZOE   Great! Now you're making fun of me. It's a poem! You're allowed to make up words.

BEN   I wasn't making fu /

ZOE   You're actually supposed to make up words.

LILITH   Isn't there another word you could have used?

ZOE   Nope. That one is perfect.

LILITH   Humour us, okay?

She takes another photo. ZOE cringes.

BEN   Why not just "I wouldn't want to step on them"?

ZOE   Boring.

BEN   Squash them?

ZOE   Predictable.

BEN   Squish?

ZOE   Doesn't rhyme.

LILITH   None of it rhymes.

ZOE   Shut UP! Why do you keep trying to make me come up with new words? What's wrong with my words?

LILITH   Why are you hiding in your father's room? What are you, a mole? *(She's taking pictures of the room.)* This place is a mess, by the way.

BEN   It's kind of pathetic.

LILITH   You have no idea!

ZOE   What I don't have is any idea what the pair of you are doing in here!!! *(She starts banging her hands against her head.)* Get OUT!

The VOICES kick in again – stronger.

BEN   Weird.

LILITH   Definitely weird.

ZOE   You're weird!

BEN   Are you afraid of something?

LILITH   A fear is a negative wish. *(She takes a photo.)*

BEN   Are you feeling guilty about something? They say guilt is about memory.

LILITH   Can you think of another way to describe the "weirds"?

ZOE   Like what?

> *She sits in the wheelchair and lights a cigarette. The VOICES go: "Aaaahhhhhhhh" in the soundscape and there is smoke. Flash – another photo.*

BEN   Harpies?

ZOE   Too mythical.

LILITH   Gorgons?

ZOE   No.

LILITH   Elves?

ZOE   I think you already decided that elves is probably what I want them to be.

LILITH   We decided that, did we? *(snapping another photo of ZOE)*

BEN   Fiends?

GENERAL   *(giving up on the hand jive, he throws his hands in the air)* What about – shades?

> *Silence as if a lightbulb just went on. Nobody moves.*

ZOE   Yeah. Shades. Shit! Nightshades. The Nightshades—all of you—the whole friggin' family. Friggin' wierds. Friggin' shades. Friggin'. Deadly. Nightshades.

l to r: John Dartt and Krista Laveck
Photo by Charlie Rhindress

Pause. No response as the whispering VOICES in the soundscape take over once again, this time, however, LILITH and BEN and the GENERAL appear to be doing the whispering (they're mouthing the words) and ZOE is watching them do it: "You're stupid. You're so stupid. You've always been a loser. You're always gonna be a loser. Loser. Loser. Loser. Lazy, selfish, self-centred, childish, stupid. Loser. Loser. Loser." *etc. As the words become clearer, it becomes obvious that they are the VOICES of the family. As they get clearer, they fade out: first the GENERAL's voice disappears from the mix, then BEN's, then LILITH's. BEN and LILITH freeze behind the scrim.*

You are the weirds!!!

Pause. Only ZOE's voice remains in the mix and it is very quiet now.

I am the weirds.

The VOICES have stopped.

Koo koo ka choo.

> *The GENERAL takes his hat from ZOE, tips it to her and puts it on.*

GENERAL   You know, Zoey, there are two branches to the Nightshade Family.

ZOE   What?

GENERAL   Yup. There's the Deadly Nightshades and the… what's the other one? Oh yeah – the Bittersweets!

ZOE   What's the difference?

GENERAL   Somebody told me that once. Can't remember. Don't know. Guess you'll just have to pick the one you like.

ZOE   What does that mean?

GENERAL   Your choice. Well, it's time for me to piss off. Gotta go. Things to do, places to go, old friends to see.

> *Whistling "The Limbo," he starts to leave.*

ZOE   Dad! Wait! *(He stops.)* I've been wanting to ask you. When you launched yourself into the St. Lawrence that time to save that guy, did you know that there was a law saying you had to do that? Did you know about the Rescue Law?

GENERAL   Well, Zoey, I don't remember. Who knows?

> *He takes the cigarette out of her hand and sticks it in his own mouth – lots of smoke fills the room.*

Maybe in the end, we all just have to rescue ourselves.

> *More smoke. He fades away. "The Chiquita Banana" song drifts in and LILITH and BEN whisper along to the words as they start to dance and juggle again, with the camera flashing.*

ZOE   Some choice.

> *ZOE watches as the lights leave LILITH and BEN and bounce from one wall/scrim to the next, so that different scenes/images appear on the scrims, like the images that are burned on your retina long after the events have*

passed. Most of the images are slightly out of focus – as if they're photos taken by LILITH while she was dancing, for instance: flowers and food at the funeral, the GENERAL blinking at the flash while hollering, the spilt milk, the plate and sandwich on the floor, ZOE under the blankets, the game of charades, the hospital bed, the wheelchair, the GENERAL's hat, BEN's lists, ZOE banging her head, BEN throwing the book against the wall, the GENERAL changing his glasses, the watch, the Carmen Miranda hat, LILITH dancing, the image of the dresser with the green eyes, BEN juggling, the scene with LILITH and the GENERAL when he can't remember her name, and ZOE's poems and other words written on the walls.

Maybe you're right, though. Maybe in the end, we do all just have to rescue ourselves.

She walks off the stage, through the house and leaves. The lights go to black.

The end.

During the curtain call, the music from "The Great Escape" is played and LILITH takes snaps of the audience.

Jenny Munday is a playwright, dramaturge, director, actor and arts administrator. She is the Artistic Director of Playwrights Atlantic Resource Centre (PARC) and is currently the Crake Fellow in Drama at Mount Allison University and Playwright-in Residence at Live Bait Theatre. She was Artistic Director of Mulgrave Road (Co-op) Theatre from 1989 to 1992, was Writer in Residence and Artistic Associate at Theatre New Brunswick and was a co-founder and Co-Artistic Director of the Comedy Asylum. Her twenty-five year career has largely been dedicated to the development of new Canadian work for the stage.

As an actor, she created many original roles in new works for playwrights' development centres across the country – from Rising Tide Theatre in Newfoundland to the Banff playRites Colony. She has also worked at Neptune Theatre, Mulgrave Road Theatre, Theatre New Brunswick, the Comedy Asylum, The Grand Theatre in London, at the National Arts Centre, at several summer theatres in Ontario and in radio, TV and film.

In 2007, Jenny was awarded a Theatre Nova Scotia Merritt Achievement Award for outstanding contribution to Theatre in Nova Scotia. She also received the inaugural Mallory Gilbert Award from the Professional Association of Canadian Theatre (PACT) and Tarragon Theatre in recognition of sustained, inspired and creative leadership in Canadian Theatre.

She is currently working on two new scripts for Live Bait Theatre.